11. 66

D0050404

BORN TO LOSE

"Bill Lee accurately depicts the inner workings of the mind of a pathological gambler. Ultimately, this is a story of hope, recovery, and perseverance in the face of seemingly insurmountable conditions. His memoir is a must-read for patients and families who are struggling with gambling problems as well as for the therapists who treat them."

—TIMOTHY W. FONG, M.D.
Co-director, UCLA Gambling Studies Program

"*Born to Lose* skillfully places the reader inside the mind of a compulsive gambler. Any gambler afflicted with this disease will find in these pages a great deal of identification along with guidelines for recovery."

—MARY HEINEMAN, C.S.W.
Author, *Losing Your Shirt*

Also by Bill Lee

Chinese Playground: A Memoir

362.25
L477Bb

BORN TO LOSE

Memoirs of a Compulsive Gambler

Bill Lee

San Diego Christian College
2100 Greenfield Drive
El Cajon, CA 92019

 HAZELDEN®

Hazelden
Center City, Minnesota 55012-0176

1-800-328-0094
1-651-213-4590 (Fax)
www.hazelden.org

©2005 by Hazelden Foundation
All rights reserved. Published 2005
Printed in the United States of America
No portion of this publication may be reproduced in any manner
without the written permission of the publisher

ISBN-13: 978-1-59285-153-9

Library of Congress Cataloging-in-Publication Data
Lee, Bill, 1954–
    Born to lose : memoirs of a compulsive gambler / Bill Lee.
      p. cm.
    ISBN 1-59285-153-3 (softcover)
    1. Lee, Bill, 1954– 2. Gamblers—United States—Biography.
  I. Title.

    HV6710.3.L44A3 2005
    362.2'5—dc22
    [B]

                        2004060943

Author's note

To preserve the anonymity both in and outside of Gamblers Anonymous (GA), names, dates, and minor details of some stories have been altered. With the exception of ESL, the company names of former employers are fictitious. Identities and some characteristics of managers and co-workers have been modified. Timelines of certain events have also been changed.

09 08 07 06 05 6 5 4 3 2 1

Cover design by David Spohn
Cover photo by Vivian Young
Typesetting by Stanton Publication Services, Inc.

As always, for

ERIC

In memory of

E. WALLACE

CONTENTS

Preface   ix
Acknowledgments   xiii

PART ONE   **MY DRUG OF CHOICE**

ONE   Home Group   3
TWO   Dark Legacy   11
THREE   Guts   28
FOUR   White-Collar Gambling   43
FIVE   Wannabe Blackjack Dealer   55
SIX   Divorce and Self-Destruction   64
SEVEN   Stock Guru   71
EIGHT   Career Crisis   75
NINE   Casino VIP   84
TEN   Switching Addictions   91
ELEVEN   Divine Intervention   108

PART TWO   THE ROAD TO RECOVERY

TWELVE   Gamblers Anonymous   119
THIRTEEN   Fallen Hero   147
FOURTEEN   Viva Las Vegas   179
FIFTEEN   Unlucky 7s   200
SIXTEEN   Hitting Rock Bottom   217
SEVENTEEN   Surrendering to GA   231
EIGHTEEN   Ella's Legacy   255

Epilogue   261
Appendix A: Step Work Notes   271
Appendix B: Directives from the
             GA Combo Book   283
About the Author   285

PREFACE

This story details my gambling addiction, which spans more than forty years and includes my fifteen-year involvement with Gamblers Anonymous (GA). To share my gambling history in detail, I thought it was important to open the doors to GA so the public can gain a better insight not only into this treacherous addiction but also into the transformation that occurs in recovery.

Compulsive gambling is often referred to as the hidden and invisible disease, because problem gamblers like myself don't show overt physical symptoms. As a GA member stated eloquently, "You don't smell cards on our breaths."

Here are some startling statistics that I came across while working on the manuscript. After you read my story, you can decide for yourself whether my lifelong struggle with gambling validates some—or perhaps most—of the data.

- The National Council on Problem Gambling estimates that compulsive gamblers annually cost American businesses $40 billion in lost wages and insurance claims.
- The American Insurance Institute estimates that 40 percent of all white-collar crime is committed by or for compulsive gamblers.
- Two of every three compulsive gamblers say they would commit a crime to cover gambling debts and/or to obtain money with which to gamble.
- A third of all prison inmates are considered compulsive gamblers.
- One of every five compulsive gamblers attempts suicide.
- One in four compulsive gamblers is involved in a traffic accident on the way to a gambling episode, and half admit they regularly speed on their way to a gambling episode.
- Participation in gambling among teenagers is growing three times as fast as among adults.
- Antidepressant medications, which are commonly prescribed to curb gambling urges, can actually pose a significant risk

for triggering mania, including gambling—
especially if the individual suffers from
manic depression, also known as bipolar
disorder.

- The dropout rate for Gamblers Anonymous
is over 90 percent.

The 1999 National Gambling Impact Study
Commission to Congress Report estimates that there
are more than 20 million pathological and problem
gamblers in the United States. Considering that for
every compulsive gambler, five others are affected
by the addiction, more than 100 million people are
impacted by gambling issues in the United States.

ACKNOWLEDGMENTS

First and foremost, I want to thank Dr. Lawrence Lanes and Dr. Elior Vas for their kindness and compassion. Also, Dr. Tricia Gibbs and Dr. Richard Gibbs, along with their wonderful staff, for their generosity and great care. In addition to my son, Eric, I'm blessed to have great friends who were there for me when times were dark and morbid. They include Wesley Leung, Miles Guyton, John Chang, Norm Burgos, Carol Liu, Amy Kroll, Thai Nguyen, and Liora Blinderman. I'm grateful to Karen Chernyaev and Kate Kjorlien at Hazelden and to Anne Running Sovik for their editing prowess. I also want to thank literary agent Susan Rabiner for her insight and guidance.

The devil invented gambling.

SAINT AUGUSTINE

PART ONE

MY DRUG OF CHOICE

ONE

HOME GROUP

I could barely keep my eyes open as I gently shook the tiny handbell at 8:03 P.M. to officially start the meeting. I had just returned home to San Francisco from a business trip, catching back-to-back "red-eye" flights and debriefing my client in Silicon Valley for most of the day. The rain outside was coming down in buckets, with pellets of hail crashing against the church's ornate windows. As members continued trampling in with their umbrellas and raincoats dripping on the carpet, I shook my head, recalling that we recently paid the pastor to have it professionally cleaned. I rang the bell a little louder to tone down the laughter coming from the back of the room. Something in my gut told me that—for better or for worse—this was not going to be a dull meeting. After all, this was my home group.

The small, yellow "combo" books that serve as the cornerstone of our recovery program were neatly laid out in front of each chair on the long conference table, and the strong aroma of coffee from the kitchen filled the air of the warm, dimly lit library. In spite of the winter storm, it looked as though we were going to have a full house. So far, I counted twenty-two heads. We would have to bring in more chairs.

As secretary of the San Francisco Friday night Gamblers Anonymous (GA) meeting, I jot down each person's first name and last initial in our official notebook as they enter the room. Our profile is more or less representative of a GA group in a culturally rich metropolitan area. On this particular evening, we had eighteen Caucasians (as far as I could tell), two Asians, one Latino, and one African American. There were nineteen males and three females. The youngest member looked to be in his midtwenties, and the oldest had just turned seventy-eight. Among gambling addicts, men outnumber women approximately five to one. Also, women tend to be closet gamblers, start gambling later in life, and have a higher incidence of dual addictions. Only 2 to 4 percent of the women in GA attend meetings regularly, so my home group's above-average female membership is something I am truly proud of.

You'd never know it, but this group of unassuming-looking citizens is made up of some pretty colorful characters. Three have been convicted of felony embezzlement, one for larceny, another for armed robbery, and more than three-quarters have committed or considered committing various crimes—all to feed their gambling addiction. Everyone present has bounced a check, faced bankruptcy, and at least contemplated suicide. More than half are recovering from multiple addictions. A few proclaim that gambling is harder to kick than heroin and crack; they don't hesitate to provide vivid details. Two are homeless and another three are mandated by court to attend. One guy is out on a pass from county jail and will be returning there at the end of the meeting. Within six months, three members will no longer be with us. They will all have died of sudden causes—one within forty-eight hours after relapsing in Reno. Profound statements made by each of them at tonight's meeting will resonate deep within me for years to come.

Downstairs, a Gam-Anon meeting is taking place, where several wives, a mother, and a live-in girlfriend of problem gamblers use the Twelve Step recovery program to learn about compulsive gambling, to heal, and to offer support to one another. All of these women share a common bond: At one time or another, their lives have been devastated because someone they loved lost himself in gambling. When compulsive gamblers hit bottom, their spouses often suffer just as much or even more, since many have been in the dark about the addiction and are suddenly forced to face it head-on when the secret is uncovered. As the responsible party in the relationship, they're left to hold the family together, financially as well as emotionally.

Gam-Anon members sometimes envy spouses of addicts in other fellowships whose drug of choice is alcohol, food, or sex. At least with those addictions, the healing can begin as soon as the addiction is in remission, whereas in gambling, the financial damage can last a lifetime and beyond. It doesn't come as a surprise that one of the wives in this group had once attempted suicide. Spouses of compulsive gamblers are three times more likely to commit suicide than the general population. Fortunately, this particular woman survived and, through Gam-Anon, learned that her husband's addiction isn't her fault. In fact, she now serves as the group's secretary, sharing her wisdom with others who are living with a compulsive gambler. She has become adept at recognizing codependent relationships and encourages spouses to stop enabling their addicted partners.

Back at my meeting, a new face was sitting to my right, fidgeting in her chair: a blond woman who appeared to be in her early forties. She reminded me of my college math professor—except that the person sitting here looked like someone who was in deep mourning. I sensed tremendous pain in her voice when she called earlier in the week to confirm the meeting time and to get directions. Her name is Rita, and she was awaiting sentencing for forging company checks, to the tune of over $150,000. Like myself, she has a weakness for blackjack. A gentleman also called yesterday and indicated that he would be attending, but he hadn't shown up yet. I glanced at the door every five minutes or so, but I know that getting to that first meeting is difficult for most compulsive gamblers. It certainly was for me.

Just before nine, we begin the therapy portion of the meeting, where a number of us take turns sharing our stories with Rita. I must have heard each member's gambling history at least a dozen times and the details do get old, but there's nothing like watching newcomers' eyes light up when they identify with someone's "share." You can never predict with whom the new member will connect. I've been around long enough to know that it's not based on race, gender, religion, or socioeconomic status. If anything, within the fellowship, opposites seem to attract. Rita is about to discover that she shares many attributes with GA members. Specifically, some of us are highly proficient at tabulating numbers and have a knack for attention to minute details. In theory, this gives us an advantage when we're gambling, whether it's counting cards in blackjack, analyzing the horses and conditions at the racetrack, studying financial reports of public companies in the stock market, maintaining players' performances for sports betting, or even monitoring the letters and numbers in bingo. Unfortunately, our addiction overrides our skills, leaving us with a false sense of superiority.

In GA (as well as other Twelve Step programs), we believe that when new members are present, they are the most important people in the room. Most problem gamblers hit rock bottom just prior to joining us for the first time. More often than not, they're consumed with guilt and hopelessness. They have run out of lies and exhausted their resources, both legal and illegal. There's no more long shot or dream world. Their low self-esteem has been validated, and they feel worthless. All the negative messages they have internalized since childhood are magnified. Their self-destructive tendencies have reached a climax. They are consumed with shame and self-hatred. Their fresh wounds remind us how insidious the disease can be. The newcomer is like a ghost from our past, making sure we don't forget how susceptible we are to our urges. The new member also offers each of us an opportunity to reach out and practice Step Twelve, which is to carry the GA message to other compulsive gamblers, both inside and outside of the fellowship. Reaching out to others is a powerful tool. Our recovery depends on it. And finally, we want to make newcomers feel as welcome as possible, because the road to recovery usually consists of a lot of bumps and detours. If they don't return next week, or if they slip down the line and return to gambling, it's important for them to know that the GA door is always open. The best way for us to ensure this is to preserve their anonymity, while maintaining a safe, nonjudgmental environment where they can share their pain and receive support.

As Roger C., our resident sports handicapper, slouched forward and recounted in his baritone voice, for the umpteenth time, how he made his first bet in high school picking the Oakland Raiders over the Philadelphia Eagles in Super Bowl XV, two members sitting directly across from one another were making funny faces and lobbing candy wrappers at each other. I tapped on the table with my knuckles to halt their juvenile behavior, which is all too common whenever you have a gathering of compulsive gamblers. Many began their addictions in their teens (much earlier in my case), which also stalled their emotional maturity. The inability to accept responsibility and to deal with everyday life issues is a major obstacle for compulsive gamblers in recovery.

As we approached ten o'clock, I announced that we had time for one last speaker. At that point, about half of the members had given therapy. As I searched the room for a volunteer, Dennis T., our treasurer, raised his hand.

"Go ahead, Dennis."

"Well, actually, I was hoping that you would share last. I think it would be helpful for Rita."

Dennis caught me off guard, as I hadn't planned on speaking. Glancing over at Rita, she cocked her head slightly and raised her eyebrows. Our newcomer had nonverbally seconded the motion. Suddenly, I felt a burst of energy shooting through my body. I sat up and took a deep breath.

"Okay . . . my name is Bill L., and I'm a recovering compulsive gambler."

"Hi, Bill!" the group shouted in unison.

"My history of gambling really began before I was born . . ."

TWO

DARK LEGACY

My mother was convinced that the men in our family were cursed by a gambling demon. The addiction can be traced back at least three generations. She had been warned by my father's relatives but not until my parents were already married. By then, it was too late.

It was common knowledge in our home that my father was sold as a young boy. I didn't learn the details until I was sixteen and got hustled in a poker game. That's when my mother confided in me that my paternal grandfather was a "sick" gambler back in China. She alluded that my father was, in fact, sold in order to cover a gambling debt. At first, I thought she was simply trying to scare me so I would stop gambling. In time, I would come to fully understand her revelation.

My father gambled most of his life. He had no idea that he had inherited the disease and would also pass the addiction along to at least one of his children. (Since 1980, the American Psychiatric Association has recognized compulsive gambling as a psychiatric disorder. Through numerous twins studies, scientists have established a genetic pre-disposition to problem gambling.) My mother didn't know how to deal with it. She worked upward of sixteen hours a day as a seamstress, guarding every penny she earned to provide for our family. In spite of her valiant efforts, she wasn't able to make ends meet. My mother was stubborn and possessed a strong will, but eventually she became emotionally bankrupt.

Money was always a point of contention in our home. Day and night, my parents argued about it in their dueling dialects of Cantonese and Toishanese, and sometimes it turned violent. The messages im-planted into my head included *Don't get sick, we can't afford doctors. Don't get hurt playing, we can't afford hospitals. Don't wear out your shoes and clothes, there's no money for them.* By the time I be-came an adult I was obsessed with money. I defined and validated myself based on how much money I earned and by my material possessions. This allowed me to feel superior to others when, in fact, I never felt like I was good enough.

I can only imagine the distress my mother felt when she became pregnant with me and had to inform my father that there would be a fifth child to feed. My parents were already overwhelmed caring for my three older sisters and my brother. As soon as he heard the news, my father knew what he needed to do. He utilized his skills as an herbalist and doctor and concocted a brew, which he coerced my mother to drink. The intent was to abort my birth. His plan backfired, and I was born on October 8, 1954, complete with numerous congenital defects. Nearly fifty years later—courtesy of my father's quackery—I am still contending with health issues that originated both pre- and post-birth. So I guess you could say that the odds were stacked against me even before my birth. Essentially, I was *born to lose.*

Onward to plan B: My parents entered into negotiations to sell me to an elderly, childless couple who lived in the neighborhood. I was only three but vividly recall how they gave me the creeps whenever they came around. I would cry and turn away whenever they tried to place their hands on me. The woman looked like a man, complete with nubs on her chin, while the husband was puny with a hunchback and spoke in a whisper. The transaction would have been disguised as a private adoption. I never knew the exact reason that I remained with my family. Whenever I inquired, I got a different answer. The last time I asked, my father claimed that he loved me too much and couldn't go through with it. I think my health problems—including a ruptured appendix when I was four, just before the paperwork was to be finalized—were the real deal breakers. Whatever the case, in time I just accepted the fact that my existence was a burden.

While other kids attended preschool, I was out shining shoes and learning to hustle on the streets. I perceived money as something that can make a person happy—or that having it goes a long way in avoiding arguments, worries, embarrassment, and a sense of failure.

My father only displayed his affection when he was drunk, but at that juncture, his behavior was inappropriate. On top of being a compulsive gambler, he was an alcoholic and a sexual predator. My father would yell out to me in his slurred speech, demanding my presence next to him at the head of the table.

"Let's see how much stronger you've gotten since I last checked," he'd say as an excuse to put his hands on me.

He would start by squeezing my biceps, but before long, he'd be caressing my entire body, spending considerable time fondling my chest. Usually by then, my mother would run interference by skillfully stepping in between us, allowing me to get away without upsetting him. But in the wee hours of the night, I often saw my father disappear into my sisters' room to satisfy his illicit urges. I convinced myself that he was just checking up on them, but everyone in the house knew he was up to no good. We were simply too afraid to speak up.

My siblings and I didn't discuss our father's behavior until we were adults and all out of the house. When one of my brothers-in-law became privy to this family secret, he never spoke to my father again; he couldn't even stand to be in the same room with him. Sometimes I wish my mother could have done more to protect us from our father, but she was battling her own vicious demons. The concept of a wife openly challenging her husband is taboo in Chinese culture. I believe my mom was in denial about a lot of the problems in our family. When my sisters became adolescents, my mother felt threatened and often accused them of trying to seduce our father. The distrust she had of her own children illustrates her low self-esteem. Many times, I could tell that she had grown tired of holding it all together and just wanted to give up by putting herself to sleep, forever. All of us kids became skilled in suicide prevention: I lost count of how many times we stopped her from jumping out the window, slashing her wrist, or

15

overdosing on sleeping pills. We had little choice but to learn to read her moods and warning signs.

The work I did in psychotherapy during and after college led me to suspect that my mother suffered from schizophrenia. It also gave me the courage to confront my brother, James, for brutalizing me while we were growing up. Four years my senior, I wanted him to know that repeatedly beating me to a bloody pulp was not what my parents had in mind when they entrusted him to watch over my sisters and me. Sure, he stepped in when someone shoved me at the playground, but I would have been better off without his intervention, since his beatings were far worse than what I faced on my own. He also enjoyed pinning me down on a regular basis and tickling me until I cried, but it didn't stop there. It's as though his sadistic nature motivated him to find out what would happen next—and next—and next. Neither the tears running down my cheeks nor my screams seemed to faze him. He only stopped when he was exhausted. After he got up and walked away, I would be left curled up on the ground with my arms pressed against my ribs. Even after I picked myself up and ran out of the house, the sensation of his probing fingers lingered. I would soon make a conscious decision to spend as much time as I could out on the streets and at the playground, where gang members and bullies there were more predictable than my crazy family.

As I reflect back on my brother's behavior, I believe that beginning around age nine he was thrown into the fire of being the guardian for my three older sisters and me while my mother worked and my father was out doing who knows what. The task of being man of the house was more than James could handle, so he ruled with an iron hand—or, more appropriately, with his fists. His inability to control his temper made him a serious contender for head ogre in the house. My father's nightly drunken behavior sometimes turned violent, so there were days when I dodged physical blows from both my father and my brother. I severed my relationship with my brother a decade ago, but I do know that he inherited a hearty taste for scotch (and on special occasions cognac) from my father.

Physically, my mother was a gorgeous woman with a youthful gleam and smooth skin who turned a lot of heads whenever she stepped out. As a small child walking hand in hand with her around the neighborhood, I was extremely protective, staring down all the men who gawked at her. But as I got older and came to terms with how unhappy she was with my father, I found myself secretly fantasizing about the men we encountered, picturing them with my mother, hoping to find someone who would treat her better.

I believe that my parents' marriage was doomed long before I was born. I think my mother came to regard my father as an enemy, someone she needed to protect her children from, someone she needed to stay a step ahead of. There's no doubt in my mind that she maintained long-term battle plans in her head. I believe it is this posture that shifted her thinking from being suicidal to being a fighter—someone who refused to let her husband destroy her spirit.

By the time I was eight years old, I would wash my hands until they bled and clean my immediate surroundings repeatedly. In my mind, everything was contaminated, including myself. The more stress there was, the more I cleaned and tidied up. Both my father and brother made fun of my habits and rituals, which were later diagnosed as obsessive compulsive disorder (OCD). I tried to suppress it, but all the willpower I mustered up couldn't make a dent.

Beginning as a toddler, I would accompany my father after dinner to various gambling parlors. This was the closest I got to spending "quality" time with him. I was regarded as my father's favorite and stuck by his side like a little puppy dog every opportunity I had. When he designated me as his gambling partner, it made me feel special.

All the venues were within a five-minute walk from our apartment in San Francisco's Chinatown. Most of them were cramped and sparsely furnished rooms behind a storefront. An old hand-me-down sofa was usually backed against a wall, and a glaring lightbulb hung over each gaming table. The only wall decorations were ruffled calendars promoting local businesses, unless you count the roaches that scurried along the floorboard. And more often than not, peeling paint dangled from the water-stained ceilings.

It was easy to distinguish between the friendly versus the high-stakes games. Tourists and other passersby who overheard the clashing and shuffling of tiles were most likely in the vicinity of a social or small-wager game where a few dollars at most exchanged hands. The hard-core parlors were hidden and usually operated by criminal groups. Escorts were typically required for admittance.

By around age seven, I became familiar with the nuances of mah-jongg as a result of watching my father play for countless hours. The game is similar to rummy, where the object is to make runs and sets with the tiles, while monitoring the strategies of the other three players. I would sit quietly behind him and peer around his shoulders. Even back then, I was fascinated by the body language of gamblers. For example, I recall one man, with thick, gray nose hair sticking out, who unconsciously sat up and cleared his throat when he held a good hand. Another pushed his eyeglasses up and crossed his arms when he was on the brink of declaring victory.

Then there were one or two who sat nervously with cigarettes dangling from the side of their mouths, with the ashes building up all the way down to the butt. I sat there in suspense, wondering if and when their ashes would drop. I once pointed in order to alert a heavyset gentleman sitting across from my father that his ashes would soon make a mess but got my hand slapped, so that was the end of that.

I constantly banged my knees against the smoky, smelly ashtray stands between each chair. When my father wasn't looking, I would delicately push the black plastic lever on the rim of the tray, dropping his lit cigarettes to the bottom receptacle. At times, he would reach for a smoke, turn around, and be greeted by my devilish grin. But when he was on a losing streak, I didn't dare mess with his Camels.

Although my father was a highly intelligent man who was well respected in the community, he was not a lucky or good gambler. There were times when I would roam around the table and compare his hand to the other players. It was usually quite pathetic. Not only was my father unlucky, his instincts regarding everyone else's strategy were usually wrong. For a man who was adept at reading people and exploiting their vulnerabilities, this didn't make sense. It wasn't until I was an adult and my own gambling got out of control (again) that it became clear to me why my father gambled: he was consumed with self-hatred and seeking escape from deep emotional pain. Losing validated his belief that he was worthless. Sadly, my own demons were even more ruthless, and I became a heavier gambler than my father ever was.

✳

I used to believe that my gambling began in my early teens. Gambling was a rite of passage among street kids in Chinatown. We mimicked high rollers by betting, smoking, cussing, and flashing wads of cash. But in reality, my addiction originated back in elementary school when I was in the third grade, around the time I witnessed my first shooting. I was eight years old and standing in the middle of a rumble between blacks and Chinese when a single shot went off, striking the victim in the abdomen. The terrifying incident may very well have been the harbinger of my gambling compulsion. There was already tremendous turmoil in my home, and now the streets that were supposed to serve as a sanctuary for me were also unsafe. As a result, I searched for activities that would allow me to escape psychologically for even short periods of time.

I attended Saint Mary's Elementary School, which was located on the same block as our apartment building. As poor as we were, my mother wanted us to go to a good school. But more important, the fact that we had to walk less than a quarter of a city block and didn't have to cross any streets provided her with peace of mind regarding our safety. The school was attended mostly by third-generation middle-class Chinese Americans, with a smattering of foreign-born kids from low-income families. Although I was second-generation Chinese American, I identified with the immigrant students more, since we were impoverished and Chinese was my first language.

I vividly recall losing my baseball cards by wagering them with classmates during recess. In one game, three or more of us each perched a card against the jagged brick wall in the schoolyard. Next, we stood behind an imaginary line and took turns flicking cards one at a time, attempting to knock the targets down. Cards that missed their mark accumulated on the ground and became part of the winnings. Whoever knocked down a card won the pot. In another game, we simply stood back and flicked our cards against the wall. The person whose card landed closest to the wall collected the other players' cards.

The morning that President Kennedy was assassinated, the nuns took their respective classes to the chapel for prayer. As my class was lining up and marching to the chapel, I sneaked out and spent the next hour wagering my cards under the stairwell. I prodded three classmates to come along, but only one had the nerve to join me.

For reasons that baffled me at the time, I refused to quit when I was ahead and chased after my cards when I lost. When it was over, more often than not I walked away empty-handed. The shame I felt was overwhelming. Under my breath, I muttered the words "loser," "stupid," and "idiot." After a short time, I would feel anxious, obsessed with getting my hands on more cards. Even back then, I desperately needed to get back in action as quickly as possible. I was nine years old, at an age when most boys would be living to play baseball or fish or go exploring, but at the time, nothing else mattered.

My brother tried to help. James gave me some of his cards and instructed me to divide my cards evenly into piles.

"You have to limit yourself to one pile per day, no matter what," James advised. So I went and made five equal piles, each bound together with a rubber band.

But I couldn't control myself. By Monday or Tuesday afternoon, I would be wiped out of cards. I would leave the school grounds without permission to go home and get more cards. Eventually, I lost my entire collection of near-mint team cards.

I learned later in Gamblers Anonymous that gambling is a progressive illness, which helped to explain how I naturally advanced from wagering cards to pitching pennies and nickels against other kids at the playground. Of course, I never regarded these activities as gambling. They were just simple games that were supposed to be fun. I just happened to be lousy at them.

By age ten, I was playing blackjack and poker against James and his friends. Our apartment building contained large alcoves in the hallway, which provided access to the fire escapes. We converted them into our private gambling dens.

I never won—not a single time. The older boys intimidated me by bluffing and seemed to know when I had good cards. They would fold, leaving me with the measly ante. I would stop when my brother stepped in and decided that I had had enough. It was just as well, since not only did I lose my money, but his buddies also liked to tease and make fun of me. The humiliation deterred me, but I simply ventured off and gambled on my own. I dreamed of returning one day and cleaning them all out.

It's amazing how dares between children can easily evolve into gambling. Once I found myself arguing with the smartest girl in my seventh-grade English class about whether we would be assigned homework over the weekend. I was certain that our teacher would make an exception and not require any reading. Karen Wong, whom I had a heavy crush on, disagreed and accused me of being a loudmouth. So in front of the entire class at Marina

Junior High School, I bet Karen fifty cents that she was wrong. Egged on by her girlfriends, Karen accepted the bet. When Mrs. Miller, our teacher, arrived, the first thing she did was collect our textbooks. School administrators were conducting surprise book inspections for inventory and damage, especially graffiti. We were informed that because the books would not be returned to us until Monday, there would not be any homework. Poor Karen was forced to turn over her lunch money. I didn't have the heart to tell her that one of the student aides in the principal's office tipped me off about the inspection. This source of mine also alerted me once about a surprise fire drill, and I took a sucker bet on that prediction as well.

When it was raining outside, the window in my classroom served as a game of chance, as my classmates and I picked individual droplets and wagered on their race to the bottom of the pane. We also looked out the window at the crosswalk and placed bets on which pedestrian would be the first to cross the street. I came up with lots of variables, including which foot the pedestrians would lead with when the signal light turned green. We also constructed racetracks at the playground using discarded milk cartons and Popsicle sticks and placed ants in their respective lanes. When I started riding in cars, filling up at the gas station provided one of my favorite games—betting on whether the pump price would stop on an even or odd digit. I also liked to watch people approach corners where a newspaper vendor conducted business and guess which person would stop and buy a paper. The action would get frenetic during morning and evening commuter rush hours. In another game, we would keep our eyes glued to the entrance of a coffee shop or restaurant and wager whether the next person to walk out would be a male or female and whether the person would turn left or right.

I secured my first legitimate job when I was twelve, working part-time at a downtown pharmacy, earning $1 per hour. In a funny way, my OCD provided some benefits. I was responsible for dusting and keeping the shelves tidy, and I did an exceptional job. The bottles and packages of vitamins, cold remedies, bandages, cosmetics, and other sundries were meticulously lined up with the front labels facing straight out. I'm sure my chores took a bit longer to complete, considering that I was obsessed with being perfect. When I became fixated on an item, I had to force myself to move on to the next row or shelf.

I wasn't allowed to touch anything behind the counter, which included an assortment of condoms and other contraceptive products. I was curious but also relieved that my boss didn't require me to stock them.

My employer regarded me as a dependable, responsible, hardworking kid. The pharmacist had no idea I was leading a double life, even at such a young age. Maintaining a secret life would become second nature to me—and convenient, to hide not only my criminal activities but my escalating gambling interests as well.

My middle school years included a lot of time gambling in alleyways and Laundromats. I funded my gambling through my job, by selling illegal fireworks, by shoplifting (and then fencing the stolen goods to merchants), by stealing from my parents, and by extorting money from other kids. I felt entitled to certain classmates' lunch money, ordering a few to make their own lunches secretly at home (including a sandwich for me), so I could take their cash. Those who didn't comply were punched in the stomach and told, "Now you don't have to worry about feeling hungry."

At age thirteen, I began suffering migraine headaches, which left me bedridden for days at a time. On top of that, I was contending with severe nosebleeds lasting an hour or longer, at least once and often twice a week. Yet all this wasn't enough to keep me out of trouble.

THREE

GUTS

Not long after I entered high school in 1970, I became a regular at Mike's Pool Hall in North Beach. There, I became skilled at nine ball, thanks in part to a seasoned hustler. He taught me things that aren't taught in schools. We fine-tuned the art of exploiting my young age against older players. My biggest wins were scored when my opponents frantically chased their losses because they didn't want to look bad losing to a smart-aleck kid. We would start off betting a few dollars per game, but by the end of the sessions, the stakes reached upward of $20. Of course, by then, I was playing with their money and parlaying my winnings. I was in control and loved every minute of it.

With a little cash in my pockets and notches on my cue stick, I started fantasizing about a career as a professional pool shark. I convinced myself that when I turned eighteen, I would be traveling throughout the country, staying in fine hotels, making easy money, and establishing a name for myself.

Naturally, school seemed like a waste of time, so my attendance was sporadic. I went when I felt like going. When I did show up for classes, I was disruptive and hostile to my teachers. A future without homework or having to slave like my mother appealed to me.

Unbeknownst to me, a group of older, experienced gamblers, including a few I had hustled in pool, got together and decided that I needed to be taught a lesson. I was barely sixteen at the time. The traumatic experience would force me to admit for the first time that I had a serious gambling problem.

It began with an invitation to participate in a private poker game. A fellow named Wayne from the pool hall offered to bring me along as his partner. The arrangement was that we would split anything we won (or lost) fifty-fifty. The regular players were big-time neighborhood gamblers, but Wayne assured me that it was a friendly game and that I could drop out at any time. I was honored to be included and knew it would raise my stock at Mike's. I never suspected a thing.

The game was held Saturday evening at nine, and it took place in a second-floor flat just a few minutes walk from the pool hall. Upon arrival, Wayne rang the bell as I stomped and wiped my feet across the doormat one at a time. After about fifteen seconds, I heard a snap at the bottom of the door as it swung open without anyone there. Our host, Kenny, was pulling a lever at the top of the stairs to maneuver the door. We had the same contraption in my home.

Kenny resembled Bruce Lee, but with a longer face and lighter complexion. I discovered that his younger brother, Jerry, was a classmate of my sister May. Although Kenny was very cordial, I could tell he was not someone you'd want to tangle with. He looked to be in his mid- to late twenties and lived in the apartment with his wife and newborn son. She was in the kitchen when we arrived but retreated to their bedroom almost immediately, and I only caught a glimpse of her back. The living room was impeccably clean with older, yet polished, rosewood furniture. The aroma of black bean sauce and ginger from dinner lingered in the air.

In addition to our host, four other guys were sitting around watching television. I recognized two of them from Mike's. Everyone seemed relaxed, carrying on small talk. All of them were in their twenties.

I sat down carefully on the sofa arm, a little nervous at first. But after a few minutes, I was anxious to get started. I kept glancing over at the card table and chairs set up in the corner near a large aquarium tank. I was hoping someone would get the hint. A few minutes later, Kenny tossed two fresh decks of cards on the table. We were ready to roll.

The first few hours were uneventful. Wayne and I took turns playing, and we were each holding our own. The cards were rotated around the table, which entitled each player to deal and name his game of choice. We were alternating between regular draw and low-ball poker, five- and seven-card stud, follow the queen, and a variation of Texas hold-'em. At one point, as the cards were being handed to me, I was tempted to call out that we were playing old maid, but knew it would have been a bad joke so I simply declared, "Five-card draw, low-ball."

As the night wore on, I became more confident. In fact, during one hand, Kenny actually complimented me on my skills when I bluffed him out to take the pot. If he was trying to convince me that I was in his league, it was working.

Around one in the morning, Wayne announced that he was leaving after the next game. He had plans to go fishing before dawn and wanted to catch a few hours of sleep. At that point, we were ahead $75, which wasn't too shabby, considering that the minimum wage at the time was around $1.65 per hour. I was disappointed that the night was coming to an end.

After we divided our winnings, Wayne suggested that I continue playing. The other guys joined in with their own words of encouragement. I was flattered, unaware that a giant, imaginary sucker was dangling above my head.

We took a break when Wayne left. As I stepped out of the bathroom, I heard the guys break out in laughter. They hushed up as soon as I walked back in. Kenny reminded everyone that his baby was sleeping in the next room.

Kenny's friend John was shuffling the cards. When he finished, John tapped the edge of the deck on the table and declared, "One dollar ante; the game is guts." John asked if I was familiar with the game and my response was an unconvincing, "Uh . . . yeah."

A month or so earlier, a few friends and I had been playing cards in an all-night Laundromat. A kid named Richie mentioned that his older brother had won over fifty bucks in one hand playing a card game called guts. Richie went on to explain that the game began with only a fifty-cent ante and no incremental betting. We all looked at each other, completely puzzled. Most of us thought he was pulling our legs, which wouldn't be the first time he tried something like that.

Richie offered to demonstrate. He suggested an ante of twenty-five cents, which each one of us ponied up. As Richie dealt three cards each to us, one at a time, he pointed out that since there were four players, the pot stood at a buck. Richie informed us that we were essentially playing three-card poker for an amount equivalent to the pot. The highest possible hand is three aces, followed by pairs; ace-high can be good enough to win, while straights and flushes have no value.

Examining my cards, I saw I was holding a king, an eight, and a two. I sat to Richie's left, so he asked me first if I was in. Richie pointed out that if I stayed in, I risked losing the amount of the pot—$1 at the time. I folded my hand. My two buddies also folded. Richie declared that as the only person remaining in the game, he took the pot.

Someone was confused and asked what would happen if Richie also folded. Richie giggled and explained that the advantage of being the dealer is that he decides last. Since no one else stayed in, the money in the pot was automatically his—no matter how good or bad his cards were. There is also a version of guts poker that requires a minimum hand, for example, a pair, in order to take the pot.

Next, Richie described the outcome if each of us stayed in. Assuming that all four of us felt we had winning hands but Richie had the best cards, three of us would lose a dollar each in addition to our ante. One player would pay Richie directly, while the other two would forfeit a dollar each to the pot. Following that scenario, the pot at the conclusion of the first hand stood at $3 (a dollar each from two players plus the initial ante). Next, Richie handed the deck (clockwise) to me. I was the designated dealer for the next hand as part of the rotation. We anted up again, so the pot for the second hand was now up to $4. Anyone who chose to stay in the next hand risked having to pay up $4. Again, Richie pointed out that I had a distinct advantage because I would be the last player to declare his intentions. If everyone else folded, I could take the pot without even having to look at my cards. When that occurred, the pot would start again with the amount of the ante. In such a situation, there is immense peer pressure from players for someone to challenge the dealer (or remaining player) so the pot won't be forfeited. Richie was correct in that there isn't any incremental betting, where players traditionally "raise" back and forth against one another. Instead, the pot just builds up at a rapid rate, determining the amount of money to be won or lost. It's called guts because you gotta have guts to stay in!

After returning home from that gambling session at the Laundromat, I had asked my brother, who was still playing poker regularly, if he had ever played guts. His curt response was, "Stay away from guts. You can't handle it." Thinking back, he was absolutely right. But as usual, I felt compelled to prove him wrong.

Nervously picking up the cards that John dealt in front of me, I found myself staring at three picture cards—a queen, a king, and a jack. *Ooh, a straight,* I thought to myself. Unsure whether Richie's explanation about straights not having any value was true, I found myself too embarrassed to ask. Two players ahead of me stayed in, so I folded, breathing a sigh of relief.

My head began spinning, trying to recall all the rules, so I didn't even notice what happened next. I just heard someone say, "Ante up." Apparently, three of the guys were in contention for the first hand. One of them paid the winner $6 (the total amount from our initial ante), while the other player forfeited his $6 to the pot. After we anted up again, the pot for the second hand totaled $18—just like that.

As the cards were being dealt, I leaned over and quietly asked Kenny if straights and flushes counted. He softly replied, "No." Kenny added that some people play for fun where a straight beats any pair and flushes are ranked above straights, but three of a kind would still be the best hand. At that point, John chimed in that he once held a three-card royal flush, but was beaten by a lousy pair of twos. The table broke out in laughter.

Over the next hour, the pot rose as high as $90. I won a few small pots, but lost over $40 on just one hand. It occurred when I was dealing and held a pair of sevens. As we went around the table, one by one, players were either tossing or slamming their cards down. Kenny sat to my right and was very quiet. When I turned to him, praying to God that he'd relinquish the pot totaling $40 to me, he just stared straight ahead, softly smacking his lips. While the guys at the table began egging Kenny on to stay in, he started shaking his head from side to side, as though he couldn't justify it. After about ten seconds, Kenny exhaled loudly and whimpered, "I'm in." The guys were ecstatic, quickly turning their focus on me. The party line they had been laying on Kenny was now directed at me. None of them had the guts to stay in, but they didn't have any problem taunting me to stick my neck out.

It didn't take long for me to decide. In my mind, my pair of sevens looked promising, considering Kenny's reluctance to remain in the game. My assumption was that he had ace-high. I laid my cards down, generating a chorus of enthusiastic "oohs" and "aahs." All eyes shifted to Kenny, awaiting his reaction. Without a peep, he gently placed three "cowboys" (kings) next to my cards—swallowing up my pair. I was in shock.

Kenny's actions in that single hand should have served as a warning to me. I was not in a friendly game. I was beginning to understand why my brother warned me about guts. This sure felt a lot different than playing with Richie. Kenny's strategy to lure me in was the first sign that he had ulterior motives. I had no idea that Kenny was making his move against me. The hustle had been launched.

Sometime after two in the morning, as Kenny took the cards to deal, he suggested that the ante be increased to $2, muttering something about the game winding down soon. No one objected.

Checking the small stack of cash in front of me, I could see that I had lost the $37 that Wayne and I won together, plus another $21, give or take a buck. That left me with about $30. Ten minutes later, I was completely cleaned out and then some. In one hand, I held a pair of aces but was beaten by another player who unfolded three nines.

Kenny began consoling me. "Don't sweat it," he said. "You're among friends. Your credit is good here. Things can turn around in a hurry. In fact, let's up the ante to $3 so we can get you back on track."

John began recording my IOUs on a piece of paper. He asked for my phone number as well as my address—information that I normally guarded. Of course, I wasn't in any position to protest.

Kenny made another strategic move when it was his turn again to deal.

"Let's play one-card guts," he declared. "If there's a tie, best suit wins."

"Huh?" I replied.

"Listen up," he said. "If four guys have aces, spade is highest; then heart; after that, diamond; club is lowest."

"Okay," I said, not wanting to appear dense.

The next half-hour was horrific as Kenny took me apart, hand by hand. The pace was incredible. There wasn't sufficient time for me to think. The pots quickly rose from scratch to $50 to $100 or more with the blink of an eye. There seemed to be an unwritten rule that I was expected to stay in no matter how strong or weak my hands were. It was also peculiar that virtually every hand came down to just Kenny and me competing for the cash.

He was all over me. When I had a king, he beat me with an ace. Then he would bluff me out of the next hand. I'd drop out, holding a queen, and Kenny would show everyone that he had won the pot with merely a three card. Eventually, he psyched me out by staying in without even looking at his card. Every time I challenged him, he made me pay dearly for it. I felt like I was playing poker while standing in quicksand.

The final two hands were, for all intents and

purposes, Kenny delivering his coup de grâce. Kenny offered to let me clear my IOUs to him by playing head-to-head, double or nothing. When it was over, my debt to him was well over $200. Everyone in the room snickered while I did a poor job acting cool. The game was so lopsided that I assumed only a fraction of the IOUs would be called—if at all. The truth is that at that juncture, I didn't have a dollar to my name.

Kenny was gracious and offered to drive me home. It was just after 4:00 A.M. When we reached my house, I casually said, "Thanks," and reached for the door handle. Suddenly, I felt a firm grip on my left forearm.

"You've got a week to come up with the money," he demanded. "And remember, this is just between you and me."

Barely making eye contact with him, I quickly turned away as my eyes began welling up. I sneaked into the house, tiptoed to my bedroom in the dark, and slipped off my jacket.

Closing the door behind me, I heard the snap of the push-button light switch and my mother trotting across the hall in her slippers. She stood outside my door and knocked gently. I didn't dare answer. Our faces were inches apart, separated by thin layers of wood. I held my breath. After about ten seconds, she retreated.

Lying in my twin bed, I tossed and turned with

images of poker hands rotating in my head. Every big pot I lost was replayed. I had no idea how I was going to pay Kenny. Hell, I couldn't even think of a way to get my hands on that much cash illegally. It was more than my mother earned at a sweatshop in a full month. I prayed to God that when I woke up, it would all be a bad dream.

My sister May, who is two years older, was the only person I confided in. The following Tuesday, with Jerry's help, she located Kenny and tried to reason with him. He did not take well to her meddling. Not only did Kenny reiterate to her my debt; he moved up the deadline. The money was now due within twenty-four hours. Now I was really in a state of panic.

That evening, I sat down with my parents in our kitchen and spilled my guts. I came clean with everything: lying, stealing money from them, shoplifting, peddling on the streets, hustling people in pool—all to feed my gambling. By the end of my long, emotional disclosure, I promised them that I would straighten up and quit gambling. My mother brought up the subject of sending me abroad to live with relatives. She was at her wit's end, convinced that I was out of control. My father wouldn't hear of it. He had already lived through the pain of being separated from his birth father, and he wasn't going to allow that to happen with me. As far as my father was concerned, as long as he could still feed and clothe his family, he would not allow any of his children—especially sons (who are valued more in the traditional Chinese culture)—to be apart from him.

My father, who was well connected to leaders of the Chinese underworld, paid a visit to Kenny's dad. Shortly thereafter, Kenny sought out my sister and changed his tune. Kenny stated that he never expected me to honor the debt. He had set me up as a favor to his buddies, who felt that I had humiliated them at the pool hall. Kenny added that he actually likes me and was simply looking out for my welfare.

I found out later that Kenny was regarded as one of the best guts poker players. It was rumored that he was the architect of the one-card version of the game.

The incident stirred debate on the street. Some of the guys at the pool hall, including a few old-time hustlers, felt that Kenny was wrong for taking advantage of me, while others whispered among themselves that I had it coming and should have taken it like a man. There was also disagreement regarding my father's role. Some thought that I got off easy, but there were others who felt Kenny was the lucky one. The controversy had more to do with complying with the code of conduct within the subculture of the streets than with the legality or morality involved. If I was truly prepared to play with the big boys and earn their respect, then I shouldn't go running to my daddy. I agree with this in principle, but who knows how Kenny would have expected me to honor the debt if I had kept this our little secret. Nevertheless, the episode halted my gambling—but only for the time being.

FOUR

WHITE-COLLAR GAMBLING

In high school, my civics teacher was an eccentric, animated man who was fascinated with the stock market. When the bell rang to begin first period, Mr. Armstrong always had his small, crew-cut head and goose neck buried in the business section of the *Chronicle*, perusing the stock tables. He mumbled to himself throughout his ritual, complete with "oohs," "aahs," and "shoots."

Midway through the semester, Mr. Armstrong's enthusiasm soared as he covered the basic concepts of the equities market. He divided the class into small groups and allotted an imaginary $1,000 for each of us to invest. Our homework assignment was to research the fundamentals of public companies and submit investment recommendations back to our respective groups. While most of the students didn't seem to know where to begin, I found myself intrigued by the analyses of price/earnings ratios, gross margins, and return on investments. For me, the stock market shared similarities to peddling goods on the streets. It was basic supply and demand, with a dose of greed thrown in.

After turning twenty-one in 1975, I was ready to play the stock market with real money. My father had an acquaintance, Lou Gong, who was the top-producing stockbroker with a leading securities firm. A short, slender man with a large balding head, Mr. Gong was a dead ringer for Mr. Magoo. Most afternoons, Mr. Gong could be seen dashing through the neighborhood, exchanging pleasantries and making sales pitches to prospective clients. He spoke nonstop while waving his arms wildly, he interrupted other people's conversations, and he continued rambling as he trotted away. Not only was he a slick salesman, Mr. Gong had an uncanny ability to recall each client's portfolio. He made a point of bragging about his notable stock picks, needling anyone who didn't follow his investment advice. Of course, Mr. Gong conveniently skipped over his recommendations that tanked.

I was working part-time as an office clerk in the

financial district, and Mr. Gong's office was located in the Transamerica Pyramid less than a block away. During my breaks, I enjoyed hanging around the brokerage firm. At first, I felt out of place and was self-conscious regarding my age and casual attire, but the environment captivated me nonetheless: electronic ticker-tape machine flashing brightly, arcane symbols and numbers crawling overhead along the wall; customers crowded around Quotron machines and shouting in order to be heard; phones ringing nonstop; and workers dashing in and out of cubicles. In time, I would note the similarities between stock brokerage offices and casinos and how the stimulants in these environments cranked up my adrenaline while impairing my judgment.

I didn't realize it at the time, but my indoctrination into the stock market provided an emotional escape during a turbulent period in my life. Beginning in 1962, I started witnessing how criminals and gangs in my neighborhood were being transformed, a change triggered by an immigration directive issued by President Kennedy that allowed refugees from China to enter the United States. Street kids from Hong Kong and Macao who settled with their families in San Francisco were more organized and ruthless. Misdemeanor crimes such as stealing hubcaps and fights ending in bloody noses were elevated to a whole new level. In 1964, the notorious Wah Ching gang (which still exists today as a powerful West

Coast criminal organization, with an estimated membership of 1,800) was formed at the playground that was my second home. I stood by helplessly as my close friends were savagely beaten and some even killed by gang members, while others were hunted by the police. Many were initiated into secret society gangs that required an allegiance for life. Although I had been part of one loose-knit street gang or another since the age of eight, I resisted joining up with any of the hard-core groups until 1975, when I was twenty-one and in college. My decision to cross the line was an act of defiance against my father, who maintained close ties to the Chinese underworld. It was my way of showing him that I could be my own man.

By 1976, the most violent Asian gang war in U.S. history was raging in San Francisco's Chinatown. Organized gangs with ties to criminal groups in China were battling to control gambling, loan sharks, extortion, fireworks sales, politics, and overall turf. The total murder count (police had been tracking the statistics since 1969) was more than forty and rising steadily. Assaults with deadly weapons, drive-by shootings, and contract hits— along with armed robberies, arson, and vandalism— were being committed almost on a daily basis. Streets, alleyways, schools, playgrounds, shops, and movie houses became open battlegrounds for teens and young adults armed with handguns and semiautomatic rifles. As the entire neighborhood was being terrorized, the police kept running into brick walls. Victims were unwilling to testify, and witnesses and others refused to cooperate due to distrust of law enforcement and fear of retribution.

One particular gang that kept the police busy had a membership of nearly 150. They took their name from the popular Chinese tale "The Water Margin," which tells of a group of Robin Hood–type outlaws in the seventeenth century who targeted corrupt government officials in China. The group lived by the motto "Chung yi," meaning "loyalty" and "righteousness." This modern-day gang, which adopted the name Chung Yi, was made up of about a dozen subgroups, one of which was particularly violent and brazen. The leader was only sixteen. After turning eighteen, he would be arrested for being the mastermind of the infamous Golden Dragon Massacre in San Francisco. Eventually, he would be convicted on five counts of first-degree murder, eleven counts of assault with deadly weapons, one count of conspiracy to commit murder, and one count of conspiracy to use deadly weapons.

For two years, from 1975 to 1977, I served as this leader's driver. The role garnered considerable respect on the streets. I reveled in the fact that people feared me. I embraced the opportunity to establish a reputation based solely on who I was—not one based on being my father's son. I became immersed in a volatile subculture where dirty looks, simple misunderstandings, an accidental bump, or chance encounters resulted in gunfire. Since most issues were quickly settled through violence, my verbal conflict-resolution skills slipped to the wayside. My life during that period was filled with a lot of mixed emotions. For instance, when a friend was murdered, I would feel sad and vulnerable one moment, but the next moment I would feel angry and invincible. In addition, I would be committing the worst sins, causing tremendous grief to others without feeling any empathy or remorse (until years later) and at the same time still believing that God was watching over me. "The Lord loves us no matter what." That's what the nuns at Saint Mary's said.

I think it's fair to say that every gang that I joined, beginning as a young boy, was a desperate search for a surrogate family. This one was no different, except that this time my involvement was a life-and-death proposition. It had an element of excitement to it that I found irresistible; I was living right on the edge. The danger bonded those of us in the gang closer together. We accepted the fact that we were at war and made up rules to suit our needs and to justify our actions.

Once again, I was living a life filled with contradictions and secrets: I was consistently on the dean's list in college, recognized for outstanding performance by my employer, becoming enamored with

Wall Street, and all the while contending with extortion, kidnappings, torture, and murders. There was no logical reason that I was exposing myself to such danger, except that the lifestyle compensated for my insecurities and provided relief from emotional pain that had been festering deep inside me. I had no idea how much psychological damage this dark view of the world would have later in my life. Ironically, I earned an exit pass when members of my own gang mistook me for a police informant following the Golden Dragon Massacre and nearly executed me. However, twenty years later, when my book *Chinese Playground* was published, my so-called blood brothers would come looking for me again.

Mr. Gong used to photocopy stock recommendations issued by his firm's research department and distribute them via mass mailing, stamped with his name and phone number in bold black ink. He also handed them out to anyone within arm's reach, including me. Before long, I opened an individual account with Mr. Gong. Being an investor had a sophisticated connotation to it. I had no idea that I was essentially entering the world's largest casino.

After reaping small profits on a few trades, my intent was to purchase shares of Polaroid Corporation common stock. Mr. Gong had another idea.

He recommended that I invest in a program known as options trading. Mr. Gong pointed out that purchasing options versus equities provided additional leverage for my limited funds. One Polaroid Corporation "call" option contract entitled me to purchase a hundred shares of its common stock at a fixed price. I confided to him that I had $800 in savings—representing all the money I had. Without batting an eye, Mr. Gong's recommendation was to invest it all on Polaroid options.

I was so excited about the potential windfall that I talked my parents into purchasing the options as well. I made a presentation to them at the dinner table, displaying my research material, and assured them that the company was a good, sound investment. The idea of being able to purchase the options instead of the stock seemed too good to be true, but we went along with Mr. Gong's advice. My parents and I knew Mr. Gong was ambitious, but we had no idea how unethical and unconscionable he was. I'm sure our quest for quick, easy money clouded our judgment. All told, my parents and I invested a total of $2,400 in Polaroid options. It was considered a fortune to us back then.

Three weeks later, I stopped by Mr. Gong's office, but he was nowhere to be found. It was Friday afternoon. When I asked another broker for help in getting a price quote on my options, he hesitated before informing me that they had expired. A few hours earlier, Polaroid's stock had dropped sharply. It closed an eighth of a point below my "strike price." The options contracts my parents and I purchased were worthless.

I was shocked to learn that my options had a limited time frame. Phil, the broker who was kind enough to assist me, explained the risks involved, after the fact. Somehow, Phil didn't seem surprised that I had been duped into purchasing the options. He suggested that I speak with Mr. Gong's boss.

I headed home in a daze. During dinner, I explained what happened to my parents. My mother went into a rage, screaming, "You're good for nothing. I can't believe I have such a stupid child." My only response was, "I know . . . I'm sorry, Mommy."

I called Mr. Gong the following Monday morning, but he wouldn't take or return my phone calls. I finally found him at his office. His only response was that he did not expect the stock to drop below the strike price, and it wouldn't help to discuss it any further. I couldn't believe that he was "shining me on." I had my own ideas for dealing with Mr. Magoo, but my father anticipated my actions and demanded that I stay away from Gong. That wasn't a problem, since I had no intention of confronting Gong myself.

About a month later, I requested a meeting with Mr. Gong's boss, a vice president at the brokerage firm. My parents tried to discourage me and didn't want any part of it. They did not want to make waves or get Gong in trouble. As far they were concerned, the money they invested was gone—end of story. My parents had no idea that contacting Gong's boss was not my first preference. My original plan called for more drastic measures. I was ready to send some of my associates to locate Gong in Chinatown, give him a good beating, and demand $1,000 from him. The extra $200 would be for my buddies. I had it all figured out. When my father confronted me, I was going to tell him that I didn't disobey him. Technically, I wasn't there.

Gong's boss, Mr. Lagomarsino, agreed to see me, but I wasn't hopeful regarding the outcome. I was ready to launch plan A immediately if he gave me the runaround.

Mr. Lagomarsino was a very distinguished-looking gentleman in his midfifties. Dressed in a tailored, gray, three-piece suit, Mr. Lagomarsino looked like he might have been an aspiring baseball or soccer player in his youth. His handshake was unforgiving. As I presented my case, he listened intently. As soon as I finished, he immediately assured me that the firm would make restitution on my loss. Mr. Lagomarsino conceded that considering my age and the fact that I never received a copy of the CBOE (Chicago Board Options Exchange) prospectus as required by the SEC (Securities and Exchange Commission), the firm didn't have much recourse. My parents hadn't received the prospectus either, and I think there's a good chance the brokerage firm would have made good on their losses as well, but they refused to pursue it. I think they were hoping this would serve as a valuable lesson for me. My parents didn't even want to discuss the outcome of my meeting with Mr. Lagomarsino.

Next, Mr. Lagomarsino informed me that Gong had resigned abruptly earlier in the week. What's more, the firm's star broker corrupted all his clients' files upon his departure. Mr. Lagomarsino casually inquired if I could be of assistance in deciphering the information. Gong had devised a sophisticated coding system so no one else would be able to access his records. The names, addresses, and telephone and social security numbers were transposed in some sophisticated fashion.

All I could do was express my sympathy. I wasn't aware of a system that Chinese folks devised to sabotage business files. Mr. Lagomarsino stood up and we shook hands. He escorted me to the elevator and held it open as I stepped in. As the doors began to close, Mr. Lagomarsino quipped, "You're going to be staying far away from options, right?"

I would come to learn that investing in the stock market was a gateway drug for me. Getting a taste of the risky yet seductive world of options trading would come back to haunt me. As ludicrous as it sounds, getting a free pass from Mr. Lagomarsino probably did me more harm than good in the long run. It would be one of many bailouts that prolonged my addiction.

Although the $800 was redeposited into my savings account, my little foray on Wall Street was enough to get me back in action. I told myself that if I were going to risk losing my money, I'd rather take my chances at the casinos. At least there, I could touch and see my cash in action.

FIVE

WANNABE
BLACKJACK DEALER

Back in the early seventies, the legal casinos closest to San Francisco were in Lake Tahoe, Nevada, approximately four hours away by car (three-and-a-half hours if you couldn't wait to place your first bet). I started patronizing them when I was eighteen. Although the minimum age was twenty-one and I probably looked no older than fifteen, it was rumored that the casinos' security guards only hassled teens who loitered. The trick was to avoid making eye contact with them and to keep placing bets.

There were plenty of stories in the neighborhood of folks who got huge payoffs playing keno or the slot machines. I didn't know anyone personally, but someone always seemed to know a guy who had a neighbor or a friend's friend who hit it big at one of the casinos. The misconception back then was that the Mob ran the establishments in all of Nevada. I was convinced that anyone who owed money to a casino faced guys named Guido or Vito who wouldn't hesitate to break a limb in order to collect. But organized crime's influence was more prevalent in Las Vegas, where they had their hands in casinos such as the Tropicana, Flamingo, Sands, Sahara, Riviera, Stardust, and Caesar's Palace. Also, Howard Hughes was instrumental in transforming the image of the gaming business in the sixties when he purchased seventeen casinos in Nevada. Subsequently, laws were changed to allow publicly held companies to own casinos, thereby "sanitizing" the industry somewhat.

My buddies and I made about two trips per year, alternating between Reno and South Lake Tahoe. Each of us brought along anywhere from $50 to $100 to gamble with. (I hid my gambling money inside my socks.) We made a habit of filling up the gas tank as soon as we arrived. All of us knew firsthand the feeling of being stranded 250 miles away from home after losing the last dollar in our pockets, with nothing but fumes in the fuel tank.

It was generally understood that we were making the excursion to have fun and to garner respect in the neighborhood. Even the die-hard gamblers I knew were somewhat realistic about their prospects of beating the casinos, going as far as joking that they were taking the trips to make their scheduled donations. Only a few guys remained relentlessly optimistic, stating upon their return that—although they lost money—it was simply a deposit, until the next trip when they would retrieve their losses and then some.

In those days, I was lucky to win once every four or five trips. When I did win, the amount didn't come close to covering the previous losses. On occasion, I would also lose my food money and would have to borrow money from my traveling companions. Returning home with empty pockets, literally, was no big deal, though. Any feelings of remorse or depression didn't last more than a day or two.

After completing my undergraduate degree in psychology in 1978, I decided to spend the summer working in Lake Tahoe as a blackjack dealer. I had been working full-time for an international engineering and construction company and was laid off in March. I thought working in a casino would be a nice departure from what I'd been doing. Besides, it seemed like a great way to earn money and have some fun. I also wanted to reward myself for working forty-plus hours per week while carrying a full load of evening college courses during the past two years. I also convinced myself that I would learn to master the game of blackjack, courtesy of my new employer.

I had never lived away from home and desperately needed a break from my parents, who seemed to be increasingly overbearing day by day. My mother and father were both traditional, and they regarded my desire for more independence as being disrespectful.

A number of casinos, including Harrah's and Harvey's, had immediate openings, and they were encouraging applicants to apply in person. So early one morning in June, I packed what I needed for a few months and bade my parents good-bye. I made up a story about driving cross-country with friends. My parents weren't happy, but I was twenty-three and ready to conquer the gaming world.

It turned out to be a very short and humiliating trip. I arrived at the parking lot of Harrah's casino just before noon. I changed into a pair of slacks and a dress shirt in the men's room and headed over to the personnel office. A little plastic sign with a clock on the glass door indicated that they were out to lunch until one o'clock.

With an hour to kill, most job applicants would probably grab a bite to eat, read a newspaper, or take a stroll along the lake. Not me. I fooled myself into thinking that I would prepare for the interview by studying the blackjack dealers up close. Yeah, right. I watched three hands at most before sitting down to try my luck. I didn't win a single hand. Thirty minutes later, I was back in my car—heading home, minus $250. The realization that I couldn't even last an hour there was disheartening.

When I walked in the house, my mother was preparing dinner. I made up a story about the trip being canceled. She grinned. My father wasn't as subtle. He giggled as soon as he walked in the door and saw me standing there. So in my quest to achieve independence from my parents, I had lost a major battle. They now had reason not to take me seriously about wanting to be my own man.

It wasn't the first time I cursed at myself and swore off the casinos, but the botched employment excursion was enough to keep me away from Nevada for over a year. I continued gambling back home on occasion, primarily at social gatherings involving immediate family and close friends. The wagering was small, so the games were fun—for a change. I recall one incident when one of my sisters really pulled one over on us.

Dorothy is the middle child and not like anyone else in the family. She is very easygoing and has never indulged in drinking, drugs, gambling, or excessive shopping. Whereas the rest of us kids are street-smart, Dorothy is quite innocent and only sees the good in people. On a Saturday, May, the fourth child and a year younger than Dorothy, organized a get-together at her home to celebrate Dorothy's twenty-seventh birthday. Following dinner on a scorching September evening, half a dozen male family members carried on the tradition of partaking in a friendly game of poker. Following a few hands, Dorothy approached the table and asked if she could join in. Typically we discouraged Dorothy from participating because she didn't know a thing about poker and would slow us down considerably, as the rules had to be explained to her—sometimes repeatedly. But in this instance, she was the guest of honor so it was difficult to exclude her.

After going over some of the do's and don'ts, we proceeded to play draw poker, where the ante was a quarter and the maximum bet was a dollar; we were keeping the wagers small to keep the game friendly. After everyone drew their cards, Dorothy had a puzzled look on her face. She innocently raised her hand as if she were in grammar school and said, "Um . . . I have a question."

"What is it?" I asked.

"Well . . . if I have four cards that are alike, is that pretty good?"

"Hell, that's four of a kind. Damn right, it's good," I replied. "It beats a straight, flush, and even full house."

"Okay," Dorothy declared. And with that, she tossed all five of her blue chips in the pile.

"Wait a minute, D.G.," I interjected, calling her by her married initials. "You can't bet $5. The limit is $1."

"Oops, sorry. Okay, I bet $1. When can I bet more?"

"Just wait," I said. "You have to see if anyone raises you."

One by one, everyone threw in their cards. Obviously, no one was in a position to challenge Dorothy.

"The pot is yours," I announced. "So, D.G., what four of a kind did you have?"

"I didn't have four of anything," she replied innocently. "I was just asking."

"Then why did you want to bet so much money?"

"Oh, isn't that what you call, um, what's the term . . . 'bluffing?'"

At that moment, I looked around the table and all the guys looked like they just got kicked in the gut.

"Shiiit . . . she just pulled a Lucille Ball on us," I said.

In September 1978, I was hired by an employment agency located in downtown San Francisco to recruit secretaries and other administrative personnel. I found a one-bedroom apartment near Golden Gate

Park and finally moved out. Since I was the last child out of the house, it wasn't easy for my parents to accept, especially my mother. She had gone from being overwhelmed with raising five children most of her adult life to watching us leave the nest one by one. She didn't seem to have a problem when my sisters got married and moved out, but my brother was her favorite, so when he left, it left a huge void in her life. From that point on, she seemed determined to do everything she could to keep me at home.

In March 1980 I met Kathy, the woman who would become my wife. About the same time, my mother suffered a psychotic episode, complete with delusions that my father was trying to kill her by planting bombs throughout the house. She was also convinced that the tenants that occupied the flat directly below them were in on the conspiracy. After receiving a call from my mother in the middle of the night, where she whispered to me in Toishanese the entire conversation, I rushed over to their house and arrived just as my mother was turning to enter her bedroom holding a ten-inch carving knife. She began screaming that she had no choice but to kill my father and then go after the downstairs neighbors.

I was between jobs at the time and was volunteering at San Francisco General Hospital's Psychiatric Emergency Services, which is where I brought my mom for evaluation. Two police officers, whom my mother believed were army soldiers sent to protect her based on a story I made up, transported us there without incident. I was terrified that we would have to drag her to the hospital kicking and screaming. With the help of a hospital colleague of mine who spoke fluent Cantonese, my mother was diagnosed as schizophrenic.

My mother was transferred to a private hospital where she remained for nearly a week. I was concerned that the facility didn't always have a bilingual staff member on duty, but my mother apparently got by with her broken English. In fact, on one occasion, around three o'clock in the morning, a male patient sneaked across the segregated hospital wings and had a rendezvous with my mother's roommate. According to the report filed, my mother appeared at the nursing station obviously agitated about something. What happened next was difficult for me to accept, since I have never heard my mother use profanity in any language, but according to the official report, my mother appeared at the counter, pointing to her room and announced, "They fucking! They fucking!"

Unfortunately, from the time she was discharged, my mother has been noncompliant about taking her antipsychotic medication. To this day, she is in denial about her illness and lives in constant fear. Ironically, after my father passed away in 1992, my mother's stress and anxiety levels seemed to improve.

SIX

DIVORCE AND
SELF-DESTRUCTION

Kathy and I got married in 1981. Our son, Eric, was born in December of the same year. By 1983, we were no longer a family. Kathy was only seventeen when we met; we married when she was eighteen, and she was only nineteen when Eric was born. Although I was seven years older than Kathy, I lacked the maturity and resolve to make a marriage work. The failure of our marriage devastated me more than anything else I had ever experienced. I had never felt so deeply rejected and worthless in my life. It was as if old demons had resurfaced, screaming that I was a burden—good for nothing and unwanted. To me, being told by Kathy that she no longer loved me was no different than my mother constantly reminding me as a child how much trouble I was and how she regretted giving birth to me. When Kathy moved out, I felt like a child being abandoned. My reaction was to mask my pain by expressing tremendous anger at Kathy and just about everyone else I came into contact with. Growing up, I had adopted a dog-eat-dog attitude from the streets, and now my marital woes left me even more bitter, especially at myself.

I couldn't eat or sleep, and I was barely functional in my job as a corporate recruiter. Within a few months, I had dwindled down to barely over one hundred pounds. Just to crawl out of bed most mornings became a monumental task. Psychotherapy didn't seem to help much. I was in too much pain to let any positive reinforcement from my therapist sink in.

Initially, I buried myself in the task of caring for Eric. When Kathy and I first separated, I had custody of Eric during the weekdays. Without a doubt, Eric's unconditional love for me was the only thing that kept me from literally going insane or wanting to kill myself. Not yet two years old, he had a way of letting me know how important I was to him. The demands of being a single parent gave me a sense of purpose. I cooked our meals and also prepared the food Eric ate at day care. An hour after dinner was reserved for our playtime. Then I'd give Eric his bath and tuck him into bed. After Eric fell asleep, I continued my chores. Dishes had to be washed, Eric's breakfast and lunch for the following day needed to be prepared, and one or two loads of laundry had to be tackled. Physically drained, my head would hit the pillow around 1:00 A.M. Although my body would be exhausted, my mind kept racing. I spent countless hours tossing and turning, mentally beating myself up for the breakup of my marriage.

When Eric was staying with his mom during the weekends, I was basically left alone to self-destruct. For better or for worse, I discovered that gambling provided relief from the emotional pain. My trips to Nevada began gradually. Twice a month, I drove to Lake Tahoe by myself. I didn't want any company. Going solo, I didn't have to be accountable to anyone.

At the casinos, my game of choice was still blackjack. It provided quick action and the most stimulation. In roulette, the ball spun around too long before landing; each roll of the dice in craps didn't necessary result in a win or loss; keno left nothing to do between games; and the slot machines seemed repetitive and boring.

There were moments when blackjack didn't provide the fix I needed. I became anxious when another player couldn't decide whether to stand pat or take a card and when the blackjack dealers re-shuffled multiple decks. While other players waited patiently, I would reach over to the next table and place a bet or two. On other occasions, I yelled for the keno runner or dashed over to the sports counter to make a $500 to $2,000 wager on a professional game. Secondhand smoke and heavy perfume from other players irritated me, but I was more concerned about whether people (in my mind) brought good or bad luck.

The pit bosses appeared amused by my impulsive behavior. Also known as shift managers, these casino staff members possess impressive skills: they can simply glance at each dealer's tray and ascertain how much the house is winning or losing per table, down to the dollar. Coins strategically inserted between chips help them tally the dollar amounts of each stack, and their ears listen acutely for dealers' announcements every time cash is deposited into the drop box.

The phrase "color change" is another announcement pit bosses stay alert for at all times. It involves customers who use chips from other casinos as well as players who exchange chips for higher or lower denominations. Pit bosses like to encourage players who are winning to exchange lower denomination chips for higher ones. The latter manipulates players to increase their wagering, which usually impairs their judgment. When pit bosses request cocktails for specific players, you can be sure that orders will be filled pronto. I've witnessed many winning streaks snapped as a result of alcohol, as players gradually lose their faculties and abandon their strategies. And for years, casinos have been accused of pumping oxygen onto the gaming floor in order to keep players awake and in action.

Over a two-month period, during my visits to Lake Tahoe, I repeatedly ran into another player who made a lasting impression on me. We sat at the same table on at least four separate occasions. She was in her midforties, with ash-blond hair, and usually wore freshly pressed designer jeans. Eventually, I would learn that her name was Sandra.

The first time I encountered Sandra, she had a small stack of twenty-five-dollar chips in front of her and she was wagering $50 per hand. The gold Rolex watch on her right wrist caught my attention. She didn't wear any rings on her fingers. We were sitting at a twenty-five-dollar (minimum) table, and my own wagers varied from $25 to $50 per hand. Within an hour, I witnessed Sandra sign three casino "markers" (checks) for $500 each. At first, I suspected that she was a shill, someone hired by the casino to pose as a player. Some casinos plant shills to keep the action going and to manipulate larger bets. After a while, they're easy to spot because dealers often double as shills.

I saw Sandra again on my next trip, two weeks later. I was moving from table to table trying to find a cold dealer and wound up sitting next to her. She avoided conversation with other players and only spoke to order a drink or to request markers. Her mood was always somber. When she was dealt good cards, including blackjacks, her expression was no different than when she was standing on sixteen.

During the Thanksgiving weekend, Sandra and I were playing against a dealer who fell into a slump. Soon every spot on the table was taken. Players were cheering loudly and exchanging high fives. Most of us began standing pat on twelve or higher. The dealer's face-up card was consistently weak, and she busted on virtually every hand. As the security guard arrived to replenish the dealer's chip tray, Sandra just sat there quietly, massaging her growing stacks of chips and clicking her nails. If anything, she appeared perturbed by all the exuberance at the table. Most of the players scrambled when the dealer was relieved and her replacement drew back-to-back blackjacks. Sandra and I didn't budge. An hour later, all my chips were gone. I got up and left as Sandra motioned for a marker by raising her left hand and making a scribbling motion.

On Christmas Eve, 1983, I was alone and

decided to drive to Lake Tahoe, arriving in the early afternoon. At around 4:30 I noticed an empty anchor (last position) chair at a twenty-five-dollar blackjack table and sat down. I looked across and saw Sandra cutting the cards at first base. She was constantly glancing at her watch. Ten minutes after I arrived, Sandra gulped down her coffee, dropped the casino chips into her Gucci purse, and dashed off toward the exit leading to the parking lot. I was left alone with Margie, one of the friendlier dealers, who gave me the scoop on Sandra.

I learned that Sandra was a high-powered attorney from New York. She had been summoned to Lake Tahoe in early October when her mother was hospitalized. The diagnosis was terminal cancer. When Sandra wasn't visiting with her mother at the hospital, she spent her spare time at the blackjack tables. Apparently, Margie was one of the few dealers whom Sandra had opened up to.

I never saw Sandra again. I thought about her on occasion, especially after I established credit at the casino and started taking out markers. In a sad way, Sandra and I were kindred spirits. We were both grieving the loss of family and seeking to numb our pain. Gambling was our common drug of choice.

SEVEN

STOCK GURU

By the end of 1983, my biweekly gambling junkets to Lake Tahoe were no longer satisfying my needs. As the custody for Eric became extremely contentious, my urges to gamble became stronger and more frequent. Whereas my preoccupation with gambling used to begin a day or two before my next excursion, it began surfacing sooner. Eventually, the urges started almost as soon as I returned home. All I could think about was getting back to the tables. It wasn't about feeling good or having fun; it was more about not feeling bad. Most of the time, I settled for not feeling anything. I needed something to get me through the workweek, so I returned to the stock market.

At the time, I was working as a college recruiter for Advanced Circuits, a leading semiconductor company in Silicon Valley. When I was hired in 1982, the compensation package included incentive stock options. Unlike the options I purchased through Mr. Gong back in 1976, employee incentive stock options (ISOs) entitled me to exercise my options and purchase the company's stock if the price rose above my grant price (established shortly after I commenced employment). No investment was required of me until I chose to exercise the options. Many of my co-workers were long-term employees and financially secure, having amassed a good portion of their fortunes from ISOs. They also purchased additional shares of our company's stock through the employee stock purchase plan as well as on the open market.

Investing in the stock market was a common pastime among employees. A number of us monitored our competitors as part of our jobs and often purchased stocks in the firms. There was no stigma or any sense of disloyalty associated with it. It was a matter of investing in an industry we understood. Reminiscent of my days in Mr. Armstrong's class, my fellow workers and I selected equities and compared the performance of our portfolios. The size of one's investments wasn't the primary issue. It was more about analyzing companies and market trends.

We were quite competitive. Individuals who made mistakes were taunted and ridiculed over lunch.

My stocks performed well. I attributed part of my success to unconventional research of our competitors. In addition to evaluating each company's fundamentals, I studied nonfinancial data such as classified employment display ads. Not only did the "laundry lists" of job openings confirm their hiring needs and expansion, but also the position descriptions often contained proprietary details on their technology, product developments, and release schedules. These information leaks occurred when human resources departments required hiring managers to complete position requisition forms. As the hiring managers complied, they included as much detail as possible so the recruiters could utilize these forms to screen and qualify résumés.

My past foray with Polaroid options also helped me gain valuable insight. I discovered that most options expire worthless and that institutional investors utilize options to hedge their holdings. As an example, money managers who are major shareholders in a company often "write" (sell) call options on the shares they own. This strategy allows them to pocket gains even if the stock price remains unchanged. Individual investors do this as well on a smaller scale.

I also noted trading patterns of certain stocks. For instance, the stock price of our main competitor dropped an average of 12 percent immediately following their quarterly earnings announcements. This occurred three consecutive quarters in a row. It didn't matter how stellar the results were. The old adage of "buy on the rumor and sell on the news" proved to be true as many money managers strove to lock in their profits each quarter. Other institutional traders preferred shifting their equities portfolios during the last week or two before the end of each quarter; this is known as "window dressing." The bottom line is that when you have several major players, such as mutual-fund money managers, accumulating or disposing of a particular stock at the same time, it often creates an imbalance in the trading volume, thereby dramatically moving the stock price up or down. My job involved traveling to universities throughout the country to recruit college graduates, a position that had its advantages. When our competitors altered their interview schedules, in some cases canceling their appearances altogether, it alerted me that they may have missed achieving their revenue targets, resulting in a hiring freeze.

Many of my co-workers began seeking my advice and emulating my stock trades, step by step. I gained a reputation of being the guru of high-tech stock trading. For about six months, my gains from the stock market made up for the thousands of dollars I had lost (and continued to lose) in the casinos. But things took a nasty turn after I was removed from my job.

EIGHT

CAREER CRISIS

In early 1984, my boss resigned, and I was appointed to manage the company's college recruiting department on an interim basis. I was assured that the promotion would become official within six months, as long as I didn't screw up.

My staff numbered six, including administrative support. Our mandate was to hire 1,200 college grads during the 1983 to 1984 recruiting period. We sought the brightest students receiving their bachelor's, master's, and Ph.D. degrees.

My department arranged interview schedules at more than fifty universities throughout the United

States. Employees from virtually every department throughout the company participated in our efforts, with the majority assigned to recruit at their alma mater. We also coordinated student co-op, internship, and mentoring programs with select schools.

Everything was going smoothly until I got a call one morning from Jim Monroe, the company's executive vice president of sales. His daughter, Laura, was graduating from Cal Poly, San Luis Obispo, and he wanted to make sure we interviewed her on our upcoming recruiting trip. According to Jim, Laura passionately wanted to work in sales, but there were a couple of problems. First, Laura couldn't get on the schedule because her grade-point average did not meet our minimum requirements. Second, our company had a firm policy against immediate family members working in the same department. So Jim asked me to monitor the disposition of Laura's employment application and ensure that an interview slot was reserved for her, while he worked on convincing our chairman to bend the rules.

First thing Monday morning, following the campus interviews at Cal Poly, I received the nastiest phone call in my career. At first, I couldn't tell who was on the other end of the line. The person was spewing four-letter words nonstop at the top of his lungs. Even after I figured out that it was Jim Monroe and tried to calm him down, it didn't do any good. All I could make out was that Laura called her mom in tears Friday night, claiming that she was turned away at the placement center. At one point, Jim screamed something about having me fired. I assured him that I would find out what happened and offered to fly Laura in for a plant interview. His reply, right before he hung up was, "It's too late, you son of a bitch. Somebody's blood has to spill, and it's gonna be yours!"

Suddenly, my defensive stance turned hostile. My heart was racing as I reached for the company telephone directory to get Jim's extension. At that point, I didn't care who he was. I just wanted to cuss back at him. I had to get the last word in. Then I thought about going over to his office and confronting him. I knew he had recently purchased a Mercedes, and the thought of kicking or "keying" his new car crossed my mind. My conflict-resolution skills were limited. I was still thinking and reacting like a street punk.

After a few minutes, I calmed down. I found myself trying to make sense of what happened. Assuming that there was a screw-up and our company representative, Pradeep, did turn Laura away, why isn't Jim taking it out on him? Apparently, I was an easier target than Pradeep, since he was a highly regarded engineer. Whatever the case, I decided to gather the facts.

It just took one phone call to uncover what happened. Pradeep fell ill shortly after lunch at Cal

Poly. He tried his best to complete the afternoon interviews but retreated to the hotel feeling feverish, shortly before three. According to Pradeep, he scribbled a note apologizing for the cancellations and posted it outside his interview room. Since returning to the office, he'd already made calls and conducted phone interviews with most of the candidates he missed on campus. He left Laura a message and was waiting to hear back from her.

I reported the incident to my boss. He mentioned it to Stan Winslow, the vice president of human resources, and eventually, the story reached the chairman. I heard that during his weekly staff meeting, the chairman openly teased Jim Monroe about trying to hire his daughter in sales. Three weeks later, Jim followed through on his threat. The worst part of it was that the person who carried out his dirty work was someone I considered a friend.

Glenn Baldwin was a sales manager whom I enjoyed working with. The first employee I recruited into the company was for Glenn's department. On many occasions, Glenn asked me to steer candidates to his group when he was competing with other internal managers. I probably obliged more often than I should have.

When Glenn left a message requesting that I call him, I didn't think much of it. He owed me a lunch, so I figured he was calling to coordinate our calendars. But when I reached him, he immediately launched into a tirade about my performance.

"Bill, two weeks ago, I specifically asked you to arrange plant interviews for two candidates from the University of Illinois: David Mattison and Jeremy Atkins. I didn't get any response from you, so I called them directly. Well, guess what? They already accepted jobs with other companies. We lost them because you didn't follow up!"

"Glenn, listen to me," I replied. "I'm not familiar with David Mattison or Jeremy—"

"No, *you* listen, Bill," Glenn interrupted. "I just sent Stan Winslow a memo notifying him that we have absolutely no confidence in you. In my opinion, you should be removed from your job!"

I reported the conversation to Stan Winslow right away, and he reassured me that my job was not in jeopardy. I inquired about David Mattison and Jeremy Atkins with the recruiter who was in charge of the University of Illinois (our chairman's alma mater), and she wasn't familiar with either of them. A few days later, Frank Baker, a human resources manager who supported one of our largest divisions, asked me if I'd like to transfer and work for him. He was vague about the job duties. Simultaneously, my boss informed me that he decided to promote someone else to manage the college recruiting department. He advised me to take the transfer, effective immediately. It wasn't even an option for me to remain in the employment group.

I had little choice but to accept the transfer. It was either that or quit without having another job lined up. I tried to make the best of it, but I was angry and disgusted about the whole mess. For the most part, I was upset at Jim and Laura for my predicament. At other times, I resented my boss and Stan Winslow for not backing me up. I also felt betrayed by Glenn. Finally, I blamed Pradeep for becoming ill and myself for not having an additional company representative at Cal Poly to back him up. None of this actually mattered, because in my mind, it was simple—*I was screwed.*

When I reported to my new job, my boss was nowhere to be found. His secretary informed me that Frank was out of town on business, followed by a two-week vacation. He didn't have an office for me, so I occupied his. After that, I moved from desk to desk, depending on who was away on business or vacation. I felt like a gypsy, drifting from one location to another.

With the exception of my psychotherapist, Ellen, who had been helping me deal with my divorce, no one outside of work had any inkling that my career was in shambles. I was too embarrassed to discuss this with family or friends.

Having been placed in a lame-duck job, I spent most days following the stock market. I scoured the

Wall Street Journal, Barron's, San Jose Mercury News, and *EE (Electronic Engineering) Times* to identify prospective firms to invest in. Initially, the research kept my mind occupied and provided a sense of purpose from the hours of nine to six. I generated detailed reports, including trading strategies that were aggressive yet fairly safe. I had aspirations of making enough money in the market to quit my job. Not a day went by that I didn't dream of walking into my boss's office and telling him, "You can take this job and shove it."

As it turned out, my grandiose dreams of financial independence by way of the stock market never materialized. Instead of following my investment plans, which required discipline and patience, I began day-trading: buying and selling the same stocks over and over in a single day. I also began shorting my firm's stock—betting that the price per share would fall—due to the contempt I held for my employer.

My life was relegated to following each tick of the stocks, with every sixteenth or eighth of a point movement determining my livelihood. The clerks at the quotes department of my brokerage firm grew impatient with my compulsive telephone calling. Out of embarrassment, I disguised my voice throughout the day to avoid their snickers and sighs.

When the closing bell rang on Fridays at 1:00 P.M., I couldn't wait until Monday morning to start trading again. The weekends couldn't end fast enough for me. Three-day holiday weekends were torture.

My obsession with the stock market was so pathetic that not even Eric escaped my exploits. Beginning as a toddler, my son displayed psychic abilities. When the phone rang, he routinely identified callers before I reached the telephone. There were times when he would announce an incoming call before the first ring. And when I bought him small gifts on occasion, he had an uncanny ability to know what was underneath the wrappings, including booby prizes. So I began a ritual of asking Eric, as I dropped him off at preschool, whether business would be up or down for the day. Depending on his response, I would take long or short positions. Eric had a great track record, but before long, he didn't want to play anymore. When I pressured him to make a prediction, he refused, leaving me to fend for my sick self. I was back to square one.

My attempts to time the market, along with the fact that I was trading on emotions, resulted in losses that eventually wiped out all my savings. So I found myself in a lame-duck job scrambling for cash to pay bills, which included the mortgage on my townhouse, child support, and fees for the attorney handling my custody case. To make matters worse, I began sneaking out of work for day and overnight trips to the casinos.

Once again, I was repeating the same old destructive pattern I'd followed throughout my life. When problems became overwhelming, I escaped by gambling. Gambling added to my financial woes, which resulted in intense feelings of panic and guilt, which led to stronger urges to gamble.

As I think back on Eric's formative years, I'm sure that my gambling had a very negative impact on him, especially when I suffered heavy losses, which was quite regularly. With the exception of placing him in day care when I was working, I never left him with babysitters—not once. I regarded my custody periods with Eric as sacred and felt that being with him was a privilege. Still, I'm sure that Eric often sensed that I was physically there but emotionally distant, as I contended with enormous guilt and self-loathing because of my gambling.

NINE

CASINO VIP

With my savings and checking accounts depleted, I funded my casino action through credit cards and an unsecured loan from my credit union. Out of desperation to recoup my earlier blackjack and stock market losses, I increased the size of my bets, and that quickly drew the attention of the pit bosses. They, in turn, alerted the folks at VIP Services. That's how I met Darlene Highland.

Darlene introduced herself to me on a Sunday afternoon, just as I was getting ready to cash in my chips. Around my age, she was petite, attractive, and extremely personable. Darlene was wearing a black tuxedo and congratulated me for a successful weekend. She knew before I did that my winnings for the weekend totaled $2,200. She also knew exactly how many minutes I'd spent at the tables, the average size of my bets, if and when I played multiple hands, and whether or not I was suspected of being a "card counter." (The card counting system, developed in the 1960s, entails tracking the ratio of 10-value cards to nonpicture cards in the deck[s]. The premise is that a deck or shoe rich with "10" cards favors players. Casinos are always on the lookout for card counters and reserve the right to ban them, but the reality is that most players, like myself, lack the patience and discipline to profit from the system. In fact, I spoke to a number of pit bosses who say they welcome players with delusions of mastering the art of card counting.)

Darlene came across as a long-lost friend and made me promise that I would call her soon. She handed me a gold-embossed business card that listed her title as Manager, VIP Services. Darlene informed me that in the future, she would gladly authorize complimentary room, food, and beverages for me.

Even though I knew there were ulterior motives behind the "comps," I relished the VIP treatment. Actually, it couldn't have come at a better time. My crushed ego from the divorce and job loss desperately needed a boost, no matter how disingenuous the pampering was. Pretending to be a big shot for a day or weekend didn't solve my problems, but it sure offered a respite.

Two weeks later, I called Darlene and informed her of my plans to be in Tahoe the following weekend. She took care of the arrangements. When I arrived, the registration clerk—upon entering my name and confirming my comp status—became extremely courteous. I settled in a beautiful room that included a small television and phone in the bathroom. I ordered up a minifeast from room service: twenty-four-ounce prime rib, baked potato, mixed vegetables, tossed green salad, soup, fried chicken with fries, biscuits, fruit salad, chocolate shake, Sprite, and decaf coffee. The room service waiter automatically arranged two settings, but I was alone and simply took a few bites of each dish. The tip alone cost me more than I would normally pay for dinner at a restaurant, but it was well worth it. All I had to do was sign for the food.

That weekend, I left with $1,100 of the casino's money, after being ahead more than $5,000. Nonetheless, it earned me back-to-back wins. More important, the whole time I was in the casino, all my troubles and worries seemed trivial. Darlene recommended that I establish a credit line with the casino, making it easier for her to authorize the comps, while offering me the convenience of signing markers instead of carrying cash.

After about six weeks of receiving comps, my

wins and losses nearly evened out. Of course, I regarded myself ahead, after factoring in the free rooms, food, and beverages, which included premium seats at headline shows. It didn't come as a surprise that when I was on a hot streak, Darlene or one of the pit bosses would ask if I would like to take a break for dinner or mention in a subtle way that the headliner concert performance was about to begin and that they could reserve tickets for me. The offers were hard to refuse since I got a kick out of being escorted to the front of the line and seated early, while other folks who had been waiting for hours watched with envy behind velour ropes.

I began dating again and invited girlfriends to spend the weekend with me in Tahoe. I wanted to impress them with my status at the casino. Instead, they were exposed to the side of me that one would describe as a "monster" and the other as a "sick bastard." I can't blame them; in fact, they let me off easy with just mild name-calling. Instead of taking Linda Wang to see Smokey Robinson as promised, I refused to stop gambling and accused her of bringing me bad luck. Victoria Lew was more perceptive. She noted that the minute we entered the casino, my demeanor completely changed. I became distant and mean. As far as Victoria was concerned, I became possessed by the devil. Both refused to put up with my verbal abuse and never spoke to me again. I rationalized the breakups by thinking that I couldn't take either of them anywhere, and it was just as well. I was free again to gamble without being interrupted or jinxed.

Things went downhill from there quickly. The $5,000 line of credit I established with the casino offered easy access to money I could not manage, let alone afford to lose. I found myself repeatedly maxed out on my limit and pleading for additional funds. Twice, I received $3,000 extensions, and I was able to recoup my losses. But it got to the point where the additional funds led to greater losses, and I found myself instructing Darlene to cancel my line of credit. I placed a note in my file that read, "I, William Lee, request that no credit be extended to me. My wagering will be on a cash-only basis. Do not accept any checks or promissory notes from me effective immediately. This request can only be withdrawn in writing and delivered by registered U.S. Mail." The last sentence served as a safeguard against any action on my part to remove the note during a gambling binge. Deep down, I knew how desperate I could become when chasing my losses.

The following month, I found myself sitting at a blackjack table nearly catatonic as the dealer scooped away the last of my chips. The $2,000 in cash I brought with me was gone. As I stepped off the stool, the cocktail waitress arrived with my club soda. I didn't even acknowledge her. She stepped aside and smiled, allowing me to walk away without further embarrassment. All I could think about was getting my money back. I tracked down the casino floor manager and requested a marker for $4,000. It didn't take much arm-twisting for him to oblige. He simply asked me to write a note amending the letter in my file. Subsequently, he approved another marker for $3,000. All told, I gambled away $9,000—my biggest loss in a single day.

At this point, my credit cards were maxed out to the tune of $18,000 and I owed $20,000 to my credit union. I called Rodney Fong, the attorney who handled my divorce, and confided in him regarding my gambling debts. I told Rodney that declaring bankruptcy seemed to be the only way out. He discouraged me, citing the importance of maintaining a good credit history. Rodney referred me to one of his colleagues in Reno, who did not mince words. He was adamant about taking legal action against the casino for breach of contract and acting in bad faith. The casino wasted no time in proposing a $3,500 settlement, representing half of the markers I signed. We presented a counterproposal, and in the end, I received a $4,000 check from my attorney after he deducted his fee. The only stipulation the casino had was that the complaint against them and terms of the settlement be kept confidential.

My decision to threaten legal action against the casino wasn't just about money or proving that the floor manager acted improperly. Deep down, I knew

I was out of control and wanted to alienate myself from the establishment. By taking an adversarial role, my intent was to wear out my welcome. It worked: I never stepped foot in that casino again. But the settlement was another bailout, leading to heavier losses down the line. I may have been within my rights to sue the casino, but I'm sure Darlene and her cohorts knew that my gambling days weren't over—not by a long shot.

TEN

SWITCHING ADDICTIONS

I knew something had to be done about my gambling. I began to ponder joining a start-up firm. The long hours required would leave little time for anything else, including gambling. My main concern was that the demands would disrupt my time with Eric.

One day, my boss approached me about returning to the college recruiting department. I was initially excited about returning to manage my old department. But that was not what he had in mind. I would be working for my replacement. Frank Baker presented it as if he were doing me a favor. When I told him that I wanted time to think it over, Frank stressed that he had had to pull a lot of strings to get me this opportunity.

So the following day, I transferred back to the department I had helped to build—working for the person who had screwed it all up. That was more than I could take. So I placed a call to ICD (International Circuit Devices), a start-up that was about to launch their IPO (initial public offering). I was surprised to learn that the management there was aware of my troubles and interested in talking with me. They had been reluctant to contact me because, off and on for the previous six months, Advanced Circuits had been accusing ICD of stealing their employees. In fact, at my first interview, ICD asked me to sign a statement that I was the one who had initiated contact with them. After two interviews in as many days, they made me a job offer. I accepted on the spot. Submitting my resignation was liberating. And although Stan Winslow and his cronies had no idea where I was heading, they had not seen the last of me.

For the first two years, I buried myself in the work of snatching the best engineers and executives for ICD. I single-handedly staffed three new divisions and helped to open up sales offices throughout the United States and in Japan, the United Kingdom, and West Germany. I raided Advanced Circuits and other competitors relentlessly. I collected cease-and-desist demand letters from Advanced Circuits' legal department as trophies, pinning them up on the wall in my office. ICD's vice presidents were all expert recruiters, and they taught me everything they knew. We didn't advertise, we eliminated all headhunter fees, we stopped offering relocation expenses (with the exception of recent college graduates), and, in most instances, we required new hires to take a pay cut. The candidates we were going after were the top performers in the industry. They didn't have updated résumés. They didn't need them. These were folks who could pick up the phone and write their own job offers. But we convinced them that they could fulfill their "silicon" dreams by joining us. If they only cared about money, we didn't want them.

It goes without saying that ICD staffed a special breed of employees: highly intelligent, high-energy, passionate, self-confident to the point of feeling invincible, results-oriented, aggressive, territorial, competitive, and willing to take risks. The ability to function on little sleep and to possess grandiose visions met the criterion for being regarded as a stellar employee. Many of these attributes (which were desired by other Silicon Valley companies as well) are characteristics of hypomania, a form of manic depression (also known as bipolar disorder). More on that later.

ICD's chairman, Jack Carson, personally signed

off on my performance reviews, and eighty-hour workweeks were the norm. Early-morning telephone calls to Europe as well as late-night calls to Asia were routine. I lived, worked, and breathed ICD— seven days a week. I averaged four hours of sleep a night and often set the alarm to wake me up after a few hours in order to participate in overseas teleconferences. I eased up on the work hours when I had custody of Eric every other week, but I was constantly on the phone conducting business from home. It got so bad that Eric, who was in preschool, would unplug the phone and hide the phone cord.

In time, I had established what's known as a war library, a collection of proprietary data on our competitors, through my extensive network of contacts in the industry. I was often privy to inside information, such as revenue figures, product launches, and planned acquisitions, which I was tempted to use for investment purposes, but the fear of going to jail for insider trading made me think twice.

For all intents and purposes, I had merely switched addictions and become a workaholic. My job served as another sanctuary for me: it provided excitement, the work consumed all my energy, and I felt important there. But it wasn't enough. The job simply masked my insecurities. Eventually, my demons resurfaced.

Two years after joining ICD, I paid off my gambling debts of nearly $40,000, thanks in part to a frugal lifestyle that allowed me to save about a quarter of my gross salary. I also realized profits by cashing in the stock options that were granted to me when I first joined the company.

But after being debt free for around six months, my gambling urges returned stronger than ever, and I began a very dangerous, secret ritual. After working thirteen- to fourteen-hour days when I didn't have custody of Eric, I found myself making the three-and-a-half to four-hour drive late at night from my office in Santa Clara to Lake Tahoe. I was as hyper as a windup toy puppy and couldn't turn myself off. I would leave the office around ten and arrive at the casino between one-thirty and two in the morning, often having stopped for gas and a quick bite to eat. I'd play as many hands of blackjack as I could up until three o'clock, when I'd jump back in the car and race home. After a quick shower, I'd get on the phone, make a few business-related calls, then head to the office once again.

I'm sure most mornings when I walked past the receptionist, I looked like one of the extras in the graveyard scene from *Night of the Living Dead,* but so did most of my colleagues who were burning themselves out by overworking. My appearance was simply par for the course, and it was easy to blend in with my co-workers.

I went for days without sleep and often dozed off behind the wheel on the freeway. My eyes would be open, but my brain was teetering on the brink of REM (rapid eye movement) sleep. I relied on the freeway lane divider bumps or blaring horns from oncoming cars to jolt me awake. On more than one occasion, I ended up in a shallow ditch or snowbank. It's a wonder I didn't kill myself or anyone else. Years later, I would meet a fellow gambler who shared that he once fell asleep on the highway and his sports car ended up totaled underneath the rear of a semitruck. He woke up in a hospital three weeks later.

I was logging more than 40,000 miles a year on my 1982 Datsun 310 GX hatchback. Driving had always been relaxing for me, and I didn't mind the solitude. I didn't feel lonely as long as I had music blaring, a specific destination, and a purpose. But the interior of my car held dark secrets. Driving back from the casinos late at night, I often punished myself for losses by slapping myself in the face and punching the side of my head while cursing at myself. From the corner of my eye, I caught the shocked look of people from passing cars who witnessed my self-abuse. They probably thought I was an escaped mental patient.

During one of these trips, I encountered a friend of my ex-wife's at a blackjack table; he saw me wagering $500 to $1,000 per hand. He had no idea that I was buried in debt (again) and playing with money I could not afford to lose. I assumed that he would honor the code among gamblers that "what happens in a casino stays in a casino." But when he returned home, he immediately told Kathy what he had witnessed. She was convinced that I wasn't being forthright with her regarding my earnings and assets and demanded an increase in Eric's child support payment. This set off a chain of events that culminated in an ugly custody and child support fight. The dispute dragged on for nearly a year, ending in a court trial involving contentious attorneys and testimonials from psychologists, Eric's day-care provider, and court-appointed mediators.

Kathy and I are like oil and water: We fought nonstop when we were married, and the fighting turned uglier following our divorce. This left Eric in the middle of a tug-of-war, feeling like he was a pawn who had no control over his life. I'm sure my OCD had a negative impact on Eric, as I was obsessed with things being in order and having as much control as possible. Eventually, the anger and resentment that Eric was harboring would be released, terrifying both Kathy and myself to the point that we turned to each other for support and answers.

The fact that I never owned snow tires or tire chains didn't stop me from driving to and from the casinos during winter storms in the Sierra Nevada

Mountains, where one to two feet of snow could fall within a matter of hours and high, gusty winds can drop visibility down to twenty-five feet before motorists know what hit them. Perhaps I was acting out my self-destructive tendencies when I circumvented vehicle inspection sites, checkpoints where inspectors make sure cars have the proper equipment for the road conditions, by driving along back roads, but I paid the price by facing the grim reaper on several occasions. The most frightening incident occurred in the early morning hours, midweek, when I was rushing back from Lake Tahoe to make an early morning meeting. My company was searching for a vice president of sales, and the chairman scheduled a conference in his office each morning at eight o'clock for a one-to-one meeting with me to discuss progress on my recruitment efforts.

It was around quarter to three and I was twenty minutes outside of Lake Tahoe, winding through a mountainous road at about six thousand feet above sea level. Narrow, single lanes in each direction did not allow for much wiggle room, and alternating low and high headlight beams from approaching vehicles pierced through the blackness of night like Jedi light sabers. As I began a steep descent, passing groves of giant sequoia, pine, cedar, and fir, I glanced up at my rearview mirror and saw nothing but darkness. As I entered a blind curve, the tires suddenly hit black ice, a near-invisible thin layer of ice that is formed on pavement when snow melts and quickly re-freezes. The car began skidding out of control. The sensation reminded me of a bumper-car ride at an amusement park. I immediately lifted my right foot to ensure that it was off both the gas and the brake pedals, but after spinning around nearly 180 degrees, I looked up and realized that the car was gliding sideways toward the edge of the cliff. It didn't take long for me to figure out that if I continued steering into the skid, the car would be airborne shortly. So I started turning (jerking was more like it) the steering wheel in different directions and came within a foot to eighteen inches of the cliff's lip, but by the grace of God, the car remained on solid ground. Still, I was not out of danger. As the vehicle began skidding in the opposite direction, I suddenly found myself heading straight into the side of the mountain. Considering for a split second that smashing into the mammoth rock may be a viable alternative to flying in the air like *Chitty Chitty Bang Bang,* I just sat there, letting nature run its haphazard course. But at the last moment, I thought to myself, *No way!* and hit the brakes and turned the steering wheel. I narrowly missed smashing into the granite. After contending with another close call with the cliff, the car finally came to a stop. The only problem was that I was back in the westbound lane—facing east.

My heart was pounding violently against my

chest, while the rest of my body felt numb, as though my soul had already floated away. Somehow, I got the car started, crossed the solid yellow line, and drove straight. I placed myself in harm's way once more by making an illegal U-turn in the middle of the road. I wasn't thinking; I just wanted to get back on the right direction leading home.

I was shell-shocked for most of the way back. I don't think the car's speed ever exceeded forty-five miles per hour. I stopped for gas somewhere along the way, but I couldn't tell you exactly where or when. I repeatedly swore off both Lake Tahoe and gambling. I regarded this incident as a warning from God to get my act together or else. To add insult to injury, I walked into the office at eight o'clock sharp only to discover that the chairman had canceled our meeting for that morning.

By the end of the workday, almost all my fingers were sore and my forearms were black-and-blue as a result of jostling with the steering wheel. Two days later, when I opened the rear door of my hatchback to load groceries, I got a vivid reminder of the incident. Tools, motor oil, recruitment folders, and tennis gear were all strewn wildly about, as though a violent tornado had passed through, picking everything up in the air and slamming it down.

At the end of the week, I told a colleague over lunch about what had happened and confided in him about the secret life I was leading. I was desperately reaching out for support; what I got in return was denial. He didn't believe me. Jerry saw me as one of the most disciplined people he'd ever met, someone who had everything going for him. Besides, he couldn't see how it was possible, based on all the hours we were putting in. Jerry didn't realize how powerless I was over my addiction. Nevertheless, I never shared my gambling woes with anyone else at ICD. Three weeks later, spring officially arrived, and I resumed my gambling junkets, switching over to Reno temporarily, where the mountain roads were wider and I didn't have to revisit the scene and deal with flashbacks of the spinout.

One afternoon, I found myself reviewing the personnel file of Steve Kaufman, who was the company's first vice president of sales. I had never met Steve, but he was a legend, known for closing big deals and snatching customers away from competitors. It was business as usual for Steve to walk in on a sales presentation and walk out with a signed contract larger than anyone anticipated, including the client.

Just before I joined ICD, it was reported that Steve had been putting in another all-nighter at the office when he suddenly bolted out of the building around two in the morning. He didn't sign out at the security-guard station as required. His office light was still on and his attaché case was lying open on a chair. Steve jumped into his muscle car and sped up the freeway, reaching 105 miles per hour. He drove straight into a concrete wall, dying instantly. It was common knowledge among the executives that Steve suffered from wide mood swings. One minute he would be bouncing off the walls, talking nonstop, and the next minute he'd be solemn and despondent. Although his death was ruled an accident, which entitled his former wife and his family to collect on his insurance policy, company officers whispered among themselves that Steve most likely took his own life.

Something caught my attention while I was snooping around Steve's file. His performance reviews looked familiar. Out of curiosity, I pulled out my file and placed it alongside Steve's. Lo and behold, our chairman had used the same words and phrases to describe our attributes: relentless, driven, dedicated, loyal, resourceful, hardworking; understands the big picture; willing to go the extra mile. The final comment in our most recent evaluations was identical: "Bill (Steve) is a key player in the future of the company." Suspecting that our chairman used glib remarks in evaluating his direct reports, I examined the reviews of other executives but found that they were quite different from Steve's and mine.

I didn't know exactly why I was snooping around Steve's file, but discovering that we shared many similar traits was more than I bargained for. It's one thing to be curious about a man who may have killed himself, but to discover a kindred spirit with that person was spooky. It left me seriously wondering whether I was heading toward the same tragic fate.

ICD's Jack Carson was the most demanding person I had ever encountered in my career (as well as my life). In his early fifties, he had a predominantly gray beard and head of hair, which made him appear at least ten years older. His ability to clear the hallways when he stomped through the corridors illustrated the fear he instilled throughout the company. Jack always seemed to be unhappy about something. He was verbally abusive and made a habit of cussing out his executives. Jack targeted two vice presidents in particular as his whipping boys, but all of his direct reports had experienced his wrath.

Periodically, Jack required all salaried employees to work a half day on Saturdays. Most of us were working from home on the weekends anyway, but he wanted us to be on the premises. He made one exception in the company. When I had custody of Eric, I was given a reprieve. Jack knew about the problems I was having with my ex and didn't want to give her any ammunition regarding the use of child care. I appreciated it, but I did my best to report to work like everyone else, bringing Eric to the office with me on Saturday mornings about once a month. Once a senior manager was absent, citing a broken water main in his home. When he was spotted playing hooky on the golf course, he was fired Monday morning on Jack's order.

Another employee was terminated around the same time. It involved an accounts payable clerk, Francine, who was caught and prosecuted for embezzling money. She altered remittance checks, making her husband the payee. Our chairman wanted to set an example, so he made sure she was arrested and handcuffed just outside the lobby. There was a lot of speculation about Francine, including a rumor that her husband had a gambling problem and owed a large sum of money to loan sharks.

We had lunch together once, and I recall that Francine was very warm and friendly, but my gut instincts told me that she was hiding something and wanted to get on my good side for ulterior reasons. We talked about juggling work, kids, and house chores, and we agreed that she had me beat, having to do laundry, cleaning, and cooking for a family of five. What surprised me was hearing that all of Francine's children were of adult age, but apparently none helped with the housework, according to her. When I inquired about her husband and whether he'd watched the Super Bowl the past weekend, Francine quickly changed the topic, as though it were a sore subject. What she seemed most interested in was my close relationship with Jack Carson. Although we had an agreement to go dutch, she took it upon herself to pay for both our lunches when I excused myself to stop in the restroom. Francine sent me a greeting card by interoffice mail the following day, telling me how much she enjoyed our conversation and to call her if I ever needed a friend. I made a mental note that Francine was an "enabler" and desperate to get on my good side. She called and left me a message after she was formally charged, but I never returned her call. As far as I was concerned, Francine's problems were above and beyond anything I could help her with. I recall thinking that her family would finally be forced to care for themselves now that she was incarcerated.

In time, I would meet other women who reminded me of Francine, wives who were sucked into the black hole of their husbands' gambling addiction. Many end up working extra jobs, lie to relatives to obtain money, and even falsify credit card and loan applications, all to "rescue" their husbands and their finances. Collectors who work for loan sharks frequently use a technique to instill fear in the wife, who generally needs to cosign on bank withdrawals or other paperwork. They barge into the home of the gambler and rough up their victim in front of the family.

If the problem gambler has loan sharks after him (female compulsive gamblers tend to stick to legal forms of gambling, such as off- and on-line casinos, as well as the stock market), it's a good indication that he has exhausted all standard forms of borrowing and is now obligated to pay enormous interest rates on loans that are often unsecured. Ironically, when the gambler cannot pay the loan sharks, these shady lenders seem to have endless ideas for the borrower to use unethical and illegal means to get the money—namely, beg, borrow, and steal.

There will always be a place for loan sharks in the world of compulsive gamblers. It's simple supply and demand. When gamblers have nowhere else to turn, they can secretly make arrangements with the local "shylock" who doesn't always require collateral and overlooks spotty job history and poor credit scores. In fact, with sports betting, bookmakers and loan sharks generally work hand in hand to provide convenient customer service. The sad truth is that compulsive gamblers, in their desperation to feed their habit, often back themselves into a corner, borrowing from one loan shark to pay another. Some resort to selling their blood plasma for a few bucks to buy lottery tickets or to bet on a horse. I've yet to hear of a compulsive gambler who used the proceeds from blood banks for food or to repay a loan shark.

In all the gambling venues I'm aware of, including racetracks (both greyhound and horses), sports bars, pool halls, licensed card clubs, and illegal gambling dens, the only place I haven't seen loan sharks openly apply their trade is in Nevada casinos. But, of course, you've got plenty of pawn shops (regarded by many as legal loan sharks) strategically located in Las Vegas, Reno, and even Carson City to meet the demand.

The newest craze is "payday loans," where individuals who are employed go to a small neighborhood store with "Cash Advance!" flashing in bright neon lights. There, they simply produce proof of employment, write a check, and receive a loan against their payroll disbursement. Although the customary interest rates for these loans range from 600 to 800 percent, some outfits (many of which accept applications on-line) charge up to $35 per week on a $100 loan. That amounts to over 1,800 percent, which is higher than even your local shylock's rate. As of this writing, there are approximately twenty thousand payday loan outlets in the United States, not counting the Internet firms. Most states allow these businesses to operate legally. In spite of the huge interest charges, patrons wrongly figure that payday loans are still cheaper than paying fees to banks for a bounced check or to credit card companies for missed payments.

ELEVEN

DIVINE INTERVENTION

"God is our creator and he is almighty," my eldest sister, Mary, declared upon returning home one afternoon from Saint Mary's Elementary School. Mary was the first to discuss religion and prayer in our home. As a toddler who never bonded with anyone or anything, I suddenly became aware of an entity that represented hope and empowerment to me. Suffering and sacrifice were acts of love. Prayer symbolized one's devotion to the Lord.

Hearing firsthand from the nuns, beginning in kindergarten, that God is more important and powerful than my parents was confusing, yet comforting. He was invisible but possessed all the qualities that were missing in my father and mother.

Early in my childhood, I accepted prayer as a forum where I negotiated with God. If I wanted him to watch over my parents and me, I had to behave and to recite my prayers day and night. I naturally turned this into one of my OCD rituals, believing that the more I prayed, the less likely that my parents would die. Most of the time, I felt that God was listening and responding to my pleas, even when I didn't hold up my end of the bargain.

Prayer was my lifeline throughout my addiction. Sadly, my acts of devotion primarily consisted of desperate cries for help:

> "God, I promise to go to church every week if I win."

> "God, please let me get even, and I'll never ask for anything else."

> "Please, God, deal me a blackjack on the next hand."

> "Come on, God, bust the dealer."

> "It's the bottom of the ninth; please help the Giants get a grand slam."

> "Please help my team cover the point spread, God."

"God, let me win my money back and I'll never gamble again."

"Come on, God, if you really exist, you'll help me win."

When I couldn't convince God to serve as my gambling ally, I turned to a host of deceased family and friends to turn my luck around: my grandfather who passed away when I was seven, a high school chum who drowned, a former girlfriend from college who was killed, gang associates who were murdered, a business executive who died of cancer, and even co-workers who had died. All of them at one time or another were subjected to my begging and empty promises of turning over a new leaf. Once, when all the National League night-baseball games I wagered on the entire week turned out in my favor, it appeared that my prayers were answered. It was probably just a coincidence, or perhaps my deceased friends took pity on me—I don't know. But there was one incident that could only be explained as *divine intervention*.

It happened around eight-thirty on a Friday evening as I was driving east on Interstate 80. Some of the folks from ICD had planned a ski trip to Tahoe, so I had a strong incentive to head to Reno in order to avoid running into any of them at the tables. It was my third trip to the casinos in nine days.

I was sleep-deprived, hungry, lonely, and fed up with the same ol', same ol'. Gambling had stopped being fun a long time ago. It was something that my body craved, and I reluctantly accommodated it. When I was in action, I didn't feel anything—good or bad. But I was tired of it all.

As I navigated one turn after another along the mountain road with another hour or so to go before the bright skyline of Reno was visible, I began speaking to God aloud.

"God, you gotta help me. I can't take this anymore. I don't want to gamble . . . I hate it. Please help me stop."

Out of desperation, I shouted, "Damn it, God, do something!"

As my heart began pounding and I pulled on the steering wheel like I was going to rip it out of the column, I screamed, "I wish this car would break down—RIGHT NOW!"

Suddenly, the engine died, as the lights on the dashboard lit up like a Christmas tree. I had never experienced anything like it. Even the music from the stereo went silent (which didn't make any sense).

Shit, I thought to myself, *I can't believe he actually did this.*

Approaching an exit, I placed the car in neutral and coasted off the freeway. The steering and brakes were tough to control, but I was able to maneuver the car to the edge of a gas station located no more than seventy to eighty yards from the off-ramp. After coming to a stop, I engaged the parking brakes and just sat there in disbelief. I didn't know what else was in store for me.

After two or three minutes, one of the station's employees, a tall, stocky black fellow, showed up to lend assistance. The guy was a dead ringer for Officer Swanny from *Sanford and Son.* The nametag on his dark-blue shirt read George. I leaped out of the car and started blurting out something about God being responsible for this, but I stopped myself, realizing how outrageous I must've sounded. So instead, I said, "God . . . am I glad to see you."

Without uttering a word, he took the lead, and I moved out of his way. As he reached through the driver's side with his right arm and turned the steering wheel, we pushed the car to the front of a repair shop where a white station wagon was hoisted high up in the air. I already had him pegged as the mechanic, based on the red rag dangling from his pants pocket, his greasy hands, and his shirttail sticking out. He also arched his back like he'd been standing in one spot for a long time. But the most compelling clue had nothing to do with his attire. I noticed that the distance the station wagon was elevated from the ground corresponded with his six-foot-two-plus frame.

"Lucky for me you're still working. So you're George?"

He didn't respond right away. But as he lifted

the hood of my car and propped it up with the metal rod, he let out a slow "Yuppp."

"There it is," he said. "Your fan belt snapped. You're lucky the engine didn't overheat."

As I leaned over to examine the frayed belt, perhaps looking for evidence of paranormal clues, George walked into the garage, looked up at the rows of belts hanging neatly along the wall, and snatched one down using a long pole with moveable grips on the end.

"That'll be thirteen for the belt and five bucks to put it on."

"Uhh, that's fine," I answered.

I was about to ask George how long I would have to wait, but before I knew it, he reappeared and made a beeline toward the car, grasping the new belt, a socket wrench, and a long metal pry bar that I figured would be used to adjust the belt's tension.

As George began working on the car, I went over the repair costs in my head. *Hmm, thirteen bucks seems high for the fan belt. But then again, five bucks seems cheap for the labor. Oh well, I guess it evens out.*

I found myself looking up at the sky, which was brightly illuminated by stars. So many of them were visible that they appeared to be jockeying for their favorite spots. I took a deep breath and reflected on my prayers being answered. There was no doubt in my mind that God was presenting a unique opportunity for me to halt this insidious addiction that had been sucking the life out of me day after day. He was extending a spiritual hand to me.

It would be nice to report that I had an epiphany from the divine incident and headed home after the car was repaired and lived happily ever after, but that was not to be. I was too sick to take God's hand. Instead, I became more anxious. George, who had been so gracious to drop what he was doing to assist me, suddenly had to put up with my nervous pacing back and forth and my judgmental stares. All I cared about was getting back on the road as soon as possible to make up for lost time resulting from that stupid prayer. It didn't matter that no more than thirty minutes had passed from the time the car broke down until George completed the repairs.

I handed George a twenty-dollar bill and told him to keep the change.

"That's not necessary," he responded.

George went to the register and returned with a crumpled dollar bill and four quarters. "You can put 'em in the slots," he said, with a hint of sarcasm. *Gee, is it that obvious that I'm on my way to do some gambling?*

Perhaps I offended him with my behavior, but I really didn't have time to deal with it. The only thing on my mind—the only thing that mattered—was getting to the casino so I could get my fix.

I turned up the stereo for the rest of the way

and avoided all prayers or conversations with God. Deep down, I knew I had disappointed him big time. I was totally at the mercy of my addiction. I had to accept the fact that not even an act of God could stop me from gambling.

The following day, after losing my last bet, I did something I had never done before—I called my therapist from the casino. I didn't reach Ellen, but I left a long message on her antiquated answering machine, describing in detail what happened to my car on the freeway and the fact that I couldn't control my urges. She had been growing more concerned about my gambling, watching helplessly as I sank deeper and deeper into my addiction.

Ellen had mentioned Gamblers Anonymous during one of our recent sessions, in the context that it might be helpful for me to check out one of their meetings. She suggested that I call their hotline. I simply shrugged and said I would think about it. I had gotten good at doing that. Sometimes I was in so much emotional pain during our sessions that I'd only grasp a small bit of what Ellen was saying. I just waited for her mouth to stop moving and gave a standard response, such as "That's a good point" or "I never looked at it that way" or "That's interesting." Half the time, I got away with it.

PART TWO

THE ROAD TO RECOVERY

TWELVE

GAMBLERS ANONYMOUS

By March 1987 three of the four founders of ICD had left the company to start new ventures. The departed founders, as well as other executives in the industry, encouraged me to resign from ICD so I could offer my services as an independent consultant.

The thought of becoming self-employed had first crossed my mind a year earlier, around the time of my annual performance and salary review. I broached the subject then with the intent of leveraging my raise. I mentioned the idea to the vice president of human resources and administration, who was the person I technically reported to on paper, and he informed Jack Carson. They quickly asked what it would take to keep me happy (I hadn't formally resigned). I suggested a quarterly bonus plan, based on meeting specific MBOs (management by objectives), and they obliged. Jack also approved additional stock options for me, creating a nice long-term incentive package for me to stay at ICD.

I took a vacation to Asia in May of 1987 and turned in my resignation when I returned to work. This time, there was no talking me out of it. Being your own boss is as American as apple pie. Besides, I was never really good at taking orders or being a team player, since I had a hard time trusting people. I worked best independently. Being a lone gun for hire suited me perfectly.

Jack was livid when he read my notice, even threatening to take me to court. He was confident that he could get an injunction slapped on me so I wouldn't be able to start my own business. Eventually, he calmed down and his shrewdness took over. Jack offered to retain me as a consultant. For a quarterly retaining fee, I would make myself available to ICD in the event they needed me. The bottom line was that I didn't have to do a thing, except refrain from recruiting anyone from the company. I recall feeling like I was engaging in extortion (again), but this time, the party paying me insisted on it.

Before I even hung the sign on my door, I had signed up three clients in addition to ICD. All of them were start-ups, and they included the two firms now headed by the three founders who'd left ICD.

The third client involved an executive with whom I had networked for years. IIis name was also Bill, and he was somewhat of a renegade. When I would call him to exchange leads, he would send me original résumés from his file, complete with cover letters addressed to his company. They were all date-stamped with his firm's name in bold ink. I would cringe, knowing very well that the paperwork was his company's property; there's also the minor detail that the applicants did not authorize him to freely circulate their résumés.

Each client agreed to pay me a retainer of $5,000, based on the fee schedule I established. The first official check I received as my own boss was in the amount of $1,500; one of the firms just happened to issue the first check for that amount as an installment, followed by a second remittance of $3,500.

As I was launching my business, my mother was doing her best to sabotage it. She had made it clear for years that her wish was for me to move back home and be the caregiver for her and my father. She wanted me to serve in the role of honorable Chinese son—the one who proudly looks after his parents until they're deceased. To help her achieve her objective, my mom tried to convince me that I didn't have what it takes to succeed and that the business world was just too brutal for me.

Furthermore, she constantly reminded me that no woman would ever be attracted to me.

My mother suffered from delusions, but she actually possessed some psychic abilities as well. Within minutes after I received my first check in the mail, she called and asked why someone issued me a check for $1,500. After recovering from the minor shock, I reminded her that I didn't want to take any personal calls during business hours. As I was putting the receiver down, she warned me that I would regret venturing off on my own. I also faintly heard some reference regarding the amount of $5,000. It seemed that the more I reminded her not to call me during business hours, the more she did it. I often felt her breathing over my shoulder. There were days when she called more than twenty-five times between the hours of nine and six. Before long, all my retainers had been remitted, and I was sitting on $20,000. I was putting in long hours to ensure that my business would succeed, and I was making good progress. In addition to helping my clients with their recruiting needs, I was also advising them on leasing office space, security issues, their business plans, establishing policies, and, of course, keeping an eye on their competitors.

Six weeks after Bill Lee & Associates was founded, I faced an interesting dilemma. It seemed that, in my exuberance to do a good job, my progress overwhelmed my clients. They had plenty of résumés to review, candidates to interview, and input from me on their businesses. Since I was used to recruiting for up to one hundred openings at a time, the fewer than ten slots that I was now "sourcing" for received a lot of personal attention. Suddenly, I found myself two steps ahead of my clients—and they needed breathing room.

"No need to call on a daily basis, Bill. You're doing a great job. Just give us some time to catch up. We'll be in touch." In other words, *Don't call us, we'll call you.*

I soon found myself in a predicament many self-employed folks face: how to manage the "down" time. Not knowing how long the lull would last also presented a challenge. Furthermore, things could have changed in a heartbeat. One phone call from any one of my clients would have set me off in ten different directions. The fact that I was still accustomed to working eighty-hour weeks was a big part of the problem.

I became a poster child for the axiom "Idle hands are the devil's workshop." I took a one-day gambling trip, rushed home, only to be disappointed; there were zero messages on my answering machine, an empty tray on the fax machine, and my mailbox filled with nothing but bills and junk mail. So I did what any warm-blooded compulsive gambler would do—I jumped in the car and headed straight back to the casinos. This go-around, I gambled for three straight days. By the time my binge ended, $3,000 of the money my clients had entrusted to me was gone. I justified what happened by telling myself, *It could have been much worse.*

But something clicked inside of me, and I began to see the severity of the situation: *In theory, my clients could ask for a portion of their money back by terminating my services and I wouldn't have it. I'm embezzling money from my own business, and if I don't stop, I could lose the rest of it—poof!—just like that.*

My dream of working for myself was in jeopardy. I was scared and feeling hopeless. At that point, my moods swung wildly, from being excited about my career to being disgusted with myself and ashamed of my gambling. The fact that my urges were out of control negated all my professional achievements. For the first time since my ex-wife left me, I felt that life was too much bother. *Maybe my car was meant to go over the cliff near Tahoe. Perhaps God was trying to save me from myself.*

The first time I dialed the 800 number, I hung up before anyone answered. I told myself that it would be better if I called from a public pay phone, to hide my identity. I don't know why I was being so paranoid. I guess I was afraid that once I made contact, the organization might start stalking me like some religious cult would. My perception was that Twelve Step programs peddle God and religion. My relationship with God was on my terms (silly me), and I wasn't interested in changing it. My ego also prevented me from admitting my weaknesses; it's one thing to discuss my issues with my therapist in the privacy of her small office, but it's another thing to open up to strangers without any guarantees that they won't judge me. I had come to value emotional safety just as much as physical safety.

I made a commitment to my therapist, Ellen, that I would call GA, find out about the program, and get a list of meetings in the area. I was going to give her a report on my fact-finding mission at our next session. Well, it was Tuesday evening and I had less than twenty-four hours to complete my task. So after dinner, I called the toll-free number and forced myself to stay on the line. As I was tapping my fingers on the kitchen counter, a woman answered the telephone, sounding out of breath.

"Hi, is this the correct number for Gamblers Anonymous?"

"Oh sure, hang on please. Ned? Come quick, it's for you. It's someone calling about GA."

Momentarily, a man came on the line; I recognized a faint Brooklyn accent in his speech. I also sensed that he was from the streets. I told him my name was Ron (which was an alias I used from time to time, beginning as a child peddling illegal fire-works in the neighborhood; the name had come in handy in recent years when I was cold-calling and sourcing candidates, as well as gathering intelligence on ICD's competitors).

After patiently listening to my story for fifteen minutes or so, Ned responded.

"Ron, your story is very familiar to me. Com-pulsive gamblers tend to be bright, successful people who started gambling fairly young and tend to hide their addiction for years. Drug addicts and alco-holics show physical signs, but we don't. We beg, borrow, steal, lie to our friends and families, face bankruptcies and even jail." (At that point, he low-ered his voice, which indicated to me that he was speaking from personal experience.)

"Listen, man, trying to do this on your own and just using willpower isn't going to cut it. Look, we gotta get you to a meeting. You'll get support from other guys goin' through the same shit. If you need a ride, I can pick you up. How's that sound?"

"I appreciate your time . . . but I don't know. Let me think about it."

"Okay, Ron, let me leave you my home number, 'cause if you call the 800 line, you probably won't get me. Listen, dude, you call me anytime and I hope you give GA a chance. You got nothin' to lose with the program."

Ned was very nice and he provided useful infor-

mation, but this disease was like a cancer spreading—
and addressing the problem seemed to infuriate it.
After I got off the phone, my urge to gamble was even
stronger. It would be another month before I called
Ned again. This time I 'fessed up my real name and
made arrangements to attend a meeting.

With meetings held every night in the Bay Area, I
met Ned on a Monday evening near the San Francisco airport. The meeting room was located on the
second floor of a Presbyterian church. My nose
tracked the scent of coffee, while my ears moved in
the direction of loud voices. The room appeared to
be a kindergarten classroom complete with low tables, small chairs, and the work of aspiring young
artists dangling from the walls.

A man wearing a blue Hawaiian shirt, beige
shorts, and sandals approached me as soon as I
walked in. He reminded me of a ticket scalper. I just
knew that it was Ned.

"Hey, you must be Ron, I mean Bill, I'm Ned . . .
gladja made it," he exclaimed in his deep voice, simultaneously extending his hand.

"Thanks," I replied, as we shook hands.

As Ned shifted his attention back to the fellow
he had been speaking with, I looked around and saw
other folks busy pushing the classroom tables and

chairs against the wall and replacing them with standard-size metal folding chairs. In future meetings, we would occasionally sit in the kiddy chairs when there wasn't time to set up the room. The first time this happened, I recall telling myself that poetic justice was being served; here we were, grown men sitting in tiny tot chairs like children, confessing our sins.

In my attempt to appear inconspicuous, I sat in the back row, directly behind a scruffy, burly man wearing a two-piece suit that didn't match. Including myself, there were a total of nine people in the room. Except for me, everyone was white; there were no women present.

Someone handed me a small, yellow booklet. The first copy I grabbed was crumbled and had numerous coffee stains on the front and back covers. When no one was looking, I switched it with the one placed on an empty chair nearby. Eventually, I slipped it in my shirt pocket. I had no idea that this book, the GA Combo Book, which contains both the recovery and unity programs, would be the most important resource for me—not only in my recovery but in all areas of my life. Merely seventeen pages, it contains answers to the questions I had been pondering for decades regarding my addiction. The last page outlines in simple terms what compulsive gamblers need to do to sustain their recovery. I have read each word and phrase of the Combo Book more than a thousand times. Each time I open it, I gain new insight, either about my disease or myself. I have yet to meet anyone who abides by the seven directives on page 17 and is still out there gambling.

A serious-looking man with broad shoulders and a mustache sat alone at a table facing us, with his back about three feet from the blackboard. He shoved a large, empty coffee can in front of him over to the side, laid out piles of paper on the table, and placed a small triangular sign on top of the can. It read "Whom You See Here, What You Hear Here, When You Leave Here, Let It Stay Here." That provided some reassurance, but I wasn't about to pour my heart out, not by a long shot.

"My name is Tim R., and I am a compulsive gambler."

"Hi Tim," reverberated through the room, startling me a little.

"Before we begin, I'd like to ask if there are any new members present."

Oh great, I knew it was a mistake to come. Maybe he won't notice me.

Ned and a few others glanced over at me. I reluctantly raised my arm up.

"Would you give us your first name and initial of your last name, please?"

"Bill . . . last initial, L."

"Hi Bill," the group called out together.

"Thanks, and welcome to GA, Bill. You may

not realize this, but you're the most important person in the room. It's new members like you who help us in the program."

As he said that, others nodded in agreement, although I wasn't sure what he meant by that.

"Okay, what we normally do here is read from the Combo Book, make announcements, take a short break, and return for the therapy portion of the meeting. Since this is your first meeting, during therapy I'm going to ask you to read and answer some questions on pages 15 and 16. Afterward, you can introduce yourself, indicate if you think you're a compulsive gambler, and share your story with us."

I had no idea that I would be the center of attention. I simply wanted to check out a meeting, not be put under the knife and dissected for everyone to see and ridicule. The word "therapy" also caught me off guard. I didn't believe anyone there was a therapist, so who was supposed to serve as the facilitator? As the literature was being read aloud, I was preoccupied with planning my escape. I was determined to make a run for it during the break. *That's it, head to the restroom and leave from there.*

They also passed around a phone list, asking members to update their contact information, including their "clean date." I was tempted to give out a bogus number or to transpose the last two numbers of my telephone, but I went ahead and wrote down the correct digits. Then I jotted down Saturday's date as the last day I placed a bet.

In addition to the Combo Book, we also read the history of GA from a red book titled *A New Beginning.* I learned that GA was founded in Los Angeles around the beginning of 1957 by a man named Jim W. who used the Alcoholics Anonymous program as a guide. I thought it was interesting that San Francisco was the first expansion meeting of GA, followed by Las Vegas.

As soon as we broke for coffee, Ned approached me, as did the majority of the members. Perhaps they read my mind, or wanted to block my exit—just in case. But everyone was congenial and respected my boundaries. They simply wanted to welcome and commend me for being there. I could tell that they were sincere and probably knew from personal experience how awkward I must feel.

Ned brought up the subject of sponsorship. He volunteered to be my temporary sponsor, serving as my mentor in the program. I agreed, without the foggiest idea of what was expected of me. I was also afraid that Ned would end up calling me day and night.

Three members got up and spoke before my name was called. The first two walked up to the front of the room, while the third guy spoke from where he was sitting. I was preoccupied with studying the questions in the Combo Book, so I didn't catch every-thing that was said. I do recall that the member who spoke from his chair was pouring his heart out, feel-ing depressed about his addiction. He mentioned being evicted and sleeping on a friend's couch. There was some mumbling, but no comment from anyone, which, I came to discover, was the format. Personal, honest revelations without feedback or in-terruptions from other members are a key compo-nent of Twelve Step programs. It allows addicts to come clean and take responsibility for their actions. Members who violate this are regarded as "taking another person's inventory" and are chastised for it. I would come to appreciate and seek out the GA meetings that maintained these principles.

By the time Tim called me, I was feeling quite anxious, as if I were about to be given an oral exam.

"Bill, why don't you go ahead and read each question, and if you feel like it, go ahead and make a short comment about each one. You can either come up to the front or stay seated, whatever's most com-fortable for you."

"All right, I think I'll stay where I am. Let's see . . . Twenty Questions* . . .

---

* The Twenty Questions of Gamblers Anonymous are reprinted from *Gamblers Anonymous* (Combo Book), revised October 2003, 15–16.

"One, did you ever lose time from work or school due to gambling? Yes, I did, both work and when I was going to school. This goes all the way back to elementary school.

"Two, has gambling ever made your home life unhappy? Yes, gambling has *always* made my home life unhappy.

"Three, did gambling affect your reputation? Yes, it did. Some acquaintances mistakenly assumed that I was a successful stockbroker or investment analyst, instead of a compulsive day-trader.

"Four, have you ever felt remorse after gambling? Yes, especially when I lost, which is most of the time.

"Five, did you ever gamble to get money with which to pay debts or otherwise solve financial difficulties? Well, yeah, because gambling *caused* these debts and financial difficulties.

"Six, did gambling cause a decrease in your ambition or efficiency? Hmmm . . . yes, I would say it did. I thought about quitting my job and just investing in the stock market. Of course, my investment track record hasn't been too good, so there's a little hitch there." At that point, laughter broke out in the room. That helped me to relax a bit.

"Okay . . . seven, after losing did you feel you must return as soon as possible and win back your losses? Yes, definitely . . . in fact, most of the time, I didn't even leave. I would demand additional credit at the casinos. But there were many times when I would drive to the bank, withdraw more money, and race back to the casinos.

"Eight, after a win did you have a strong urge to return and win more? Oh yeah, I'd come home and all I could think of was going back and winning more. Of course, I'd just end up giving it all back and then some." At that point, from the corner of my eyes, I saw a few heads nodding in agreement.

"Nine, did you often gamble until your last dollar was gone? Yes, that's why I used to fill up my gas tank when I arrived, so I wouldn't get stranded like I had done before. But it has gone beyond losing my last dollar. I went overboard on signing markers to the casinos, to the point of requesting that no credit be extended to me. I ended up in a legal mess with one casino . . . well, that's a long story. Let's see . . . where was I?

"Ten, did you ever borrow to finance your gambling? Yes, I think I just answered that.

"Eleven, have you ever sold anything to finance gambling? Hmmm . . . let's see . . . oh yeah, I used to shoplift and sold the merchandise for gambling money. Once, I sold my record collection so I could play poker. I also sold illegal fireworks when I was young and used the proceeds for gambling. Oh, and I sold stock investments in order to pay gambling debts.

"Twelve, were you reluctant to use 'gambling

money' for normal expenditures? Definitely. Gambling was more important than buying food, clothes, paying the mortgage or utilities."

Right then, someone got up and left the room. I didn't know if I bored him or said something wrong.

"Thirteen, did gambling make you careless of the welfare of yourself and your family? Yes, it did. I didn't care if I ate or slept—because gambling came first. I also put myself at risk by driving in snow without chains and also by falling asleep at the wheel.

"Fourteen, did you ever gamble longer than you had planned? This is an easy one. Of course I did. I always gambled longer than I had planned. And as often as I could, I made sure I didn't have anywhere else to go so I could gamble without any time restrictions.

"Fifteen, have you ever gambled to escape worry or trouble? That's a funny question . . . I think that's *the* reason I gamble: to escape worry or trouble."

"Is that a yes, then?" Tim asked, as he was scribbling in a notebook.

"Yes, it is. Sorry about that. Moving along here . . .

"Sixteen, have you every committed, or considered committing, an illegal act to finance gambling? Hell yes! I've been committing crimes for gambling money since I was a young boy. And recently, I was tempted to use inside information to make money in the stock market.

"Seventeen, did gambling cause you to have difficulty in sleeping? Yep, after I gambled and tried to sleep, I kept seeing cards flashing when I closed my eyes. I have also tossed and turned worrying about all the money that I owed.

"Eighteen, do arguments, disappointments or frustrations create within you an urge to gamble? Yes, all of them do. I know that gambling is an escape for me.

"Nineteen, did you ever have an urge to celebrate any good fortune by a few hours of gambling? Sure, I use any excuse to gamble.

"Twenty, have you ever considered self-destruction as a result of your gambling? Yes, I've physically and mentally punished myself after losing." *I avoided going into details.* (A few years later, GA would revise the last question to read "Have you ever considered self-destruction *or suicide* as a result of your gambling?" I would respond an unequivocal "yes" to that as well.)

"Well, congratulations Bill, most compulsive gamblers will answer yes to at least seven of these questions. You scored a perfect twenty out of twenty. It seems like you're in the right place. Please go ahead and introduce yourself and tell us if *you* consider yourself a compulsive gambler and what brought you here tonight."

"Okay, my name is Bill L., and I do believe that I am a compulsive gambler."

"Hi Bill!" the members shouted, this time even louder than before.

As I collected my thoughts before speaking, the room turned dead silent. As I shared my story, about half the members listened intently with their eyes glued on me, while the rest seemed to take my words and drift off into their own worlds. I described a little bit about my upbringing, divorce, and career, concluding with my recent successful transition to being self-employed. Looking back at it now, I was so insecure that my first "share" in GA was far from what I would consider heartfelt; it was more of an egotistical rant that hid my pain and fears. I was preoccupied with trying to impress them.

"Give the program ninety days," Tim said. "You've got nothing to lose. If you don't see any improvement, the action will still be there for you. The casinos aren't going anywhere. In GA, we believe that compulsive gamblers who stay out there either end up dead, in jail, or insane. I really hope you'll give the program a try. Be sure to take a Combo Book and also a copy of our phone list. Have you hooked up with a temporary sponsor?"

"I've got it covered," declared Ned.

"Great, let's join hands for the Serenity Prayer. We could also use some help cleaning up afterward. Ned, why don't you lead us in the prayer."

We all stood up and the members on each side of me grabbed my hand and bowed their heads. I naturally pulled back a little. I wasn't used to holding other men's hands. I avoided eye contact with everyone; instead, I studied the shoes everyone was wearing. Ned recited some prayer I had never heard before, and it was the first reference to God I heard all night. I would learn to appreciate the Serenity Prayer and adopt it in my daily life.

A few members came up to me afterward to extend their greetings. "Try to make ninety meetings in ninety days," one preached, while another recommended Step meetings. I also heard the phrase "Take what you can, and leave the rest." I had no idea what they were talking about, nor did I care. I just wanted out of there—in a flash.

Driving home, my mind was consumed with negative thoughts. *What a bunch of losers, whining and holding hands praying. I'm not like them, and I sure as hell don't need them.* I regretted adding my telephone number to their list and thought about calling the phone company and having my number changed.

It would be nearly ten years before I would come to truly appreciate the members in GA and acknowledge that what really bothered me was recognizing my own frailties in them. Listening to other members open up was like having a mirror placed in front of me; I resented being reminded of my addiction and the problems that it created. I also discovered that my initial reaction to GA was typical. Most compulsive gamblers walk into their first meeting with a chip on their shoulders and don't give much credence to the members or the program. Those who have been arm-twisted into attending—by a judge, boss, spouse, friend, family member, or even a psychotherapist (like yours truly)—tend to be even more skeptical and guarded (more on this later). Many have been known to be disruptive and even use the program to solicit members to gamble or run a scam. I would come to regard these members, including a few in my home group, as the GA Mafia.

The GA Mafia was composed of a small number of guys who were longtime members, some with years of abstaining from gambling (according to them), who were just real pieces of work. They made up their own rules in running meetings, lent money to other members (a big no-no, regarded as bailouts), peddled drugs, stole money from the program, and used the meeting times as an excuse to rendezvous with hookers and act out their secret lives. On many occasions, members, including myself, have been locked out of meetings because one of them was out screwing around. From time to time, one of the mafia wives would show up to check up on the husband and his cover would be blown. The GA Mafia taught me that there's a big difference between abstinence and working the program. Years or decades of clean time are not necessarily an accurate measure of a person's recovery. In fact, it may give a false sense of security to addicts and their loved ones.

✳

Weeks passed and I hadn't heard a peep from Ned. I had mixed feelings about it. Initially dreading that he would call, I began to wonder why I hadn't heard from him. *Isn't that what a sponsor does?* After my first GA meeting, I made two additional trips to the casinos. I noticed that my urges actually increased after my indoctrination to GA; that gave me another excuse to avoid the fellowship, as Twelve Step groups are affectionately known.

My second meeting was, in some ways, tougher than the first. I knew where to go and didn't need any prodding from Ned, but I wasn't looking forward to walking in and admitting that I slipped and gambled. It was like acknowledging that I was weak—and that other members were better than me. I told myself that if anyone looked at me wrong or made a snide remark, I would walk out. But it wasn't bad at all. No one criticized me for gambling.

One detail that I noted was that all the members who read aloud did so eloquently, just as in the first meeting I attended. Today, I can say with pride that the best readers I have encountered are in GA meetings. Compulsive gamblers are known to be of high intelligence, so I guess it shouldn't come as a surprise how literate we are as a group.

I didn't see Ned, so I asked the secretary, Tim, to be my sponsor also and he agreed. In some circles of GA, there is a running joke that if you want to make sure a certain member doesn't call you, ask him (or her) to be your sponsor. It basically reflects the difficulties many compulsive gamblers face in taking on responsibilities, especially when it involves another person. Most of us have our hands full working our own recovery; serving as another member's guardian on top of that can be overwhelming. There isn't a test to determine when a member is ready to be a sponsor. From my experience and observation, I've seen members come alive in their recovery as soon as they become a role model for a "sponsee." But I have also seen others buckle under due to external pressures. It's worth noting that compulsive gamblers tend to be loners to begin with.

Looking back, I believe that I relied on my skills in reading people to subconsciously select what I considered at the time to be "safe" sponsors—individuals who would not contact me or expect anything of me. Tim never called me; he didn't even return my calls (not for the first fourteen years anyway). Years later, he would be elected as a GA trustee for our area, a coveted position in the fellowship, and on one of his communication letters to members, he emphasized the importance of reaching out and making calls to other members. When I read that, all I could do was grin.

At my third meeting, I used my therapy time to openly question the Combo Book, making a point that I have a writing background and would like to submit my ideas for revising the book. I was told after the meeting by a longtime member to be patient and not to be concerned about anything for the first ninety days except attending meetings. It was a polite way of saying, "Keep your mouth shut, kid; just listen and observe." I soon realized that I was simply frightened and trying to control my recovery. I was quite intimidated by the fellowship and was rebelling against it. As time went on, I would watch as new members took issue with the Combo Book and also referred to members of the fellowship as a bunch of losers; these comments would ring a loud bell in my head.

By the third month, I started attending meetings on a weekly basis, not just once every two to three weeks. Although I hadn't gambled since after my first meeting, I was still battling urges and came to the conclusion that my addiction was reacting to GA like bacteria to antibiotics; the urge could be killed during the meeting, but the aftereffect was to make it stronger and more resistant. That's why making ninety meetings in ninety days, as many members encouraged me to do, seemed like a frightening proposition. I was still skeptical about the program and probably would have given up on GA if it weren't for Ellen encouraging me to give the fellowship time. Besides, as a fellow member stated, "GA is the only [recovery] game in town," which is true. I wasn't aware of any other support group or treatment in the Bay Area.

I started using the phone list. Unfortunately, I wasn't in a place where I could offer support to anyone; I was constantly needy and calling other members for help. Virtually everyone I spoke to in the program preached "One day at a time" as though it were a mantra. I started adopting the phrase as well, repeating it over and over throughout the day. Unfortunately, I learned the hard way that sometimes we have to break it down further—to minutes and even seconds.

One evening, after returning home from a meeting, I was fighting strong urges and feeling vulnerable. I had accumulated eighty-nine days of clean time and was nervous about making ninety days for the first time. I went down the phone list and got ahold of four members, spending about half an hour with each of them. They had very different styles in response to my call for help. The first member asked me to take out the Combo Book, and he referred to different sections of it, reminding me to adhere to everything mentioned on page 17. The second person I spoke with didn't say much at all. He was a good listener, pointing out at the end of our conversation that I needed to make it to more meetings; that the one meeting per week I was attending may not be sufficient. Next, I reached a member named Doris, and she emphasized the importance of staying in close communication with my sponsor. Then she proceeded to tell me in great detail how difficult it is for her to work the program, and how she has difficulties accepting the fact that she will always be an addict. Doris's game of choice was bingo, and she let me know that she misses being able to drown her loneliness and troubles by playing four, five, and up to six cards simultaneously. The discussion with Doris distracted me from my problems, but I couldn't wait to get off the phone with her, since it was hard to get a word in throughout our telephone conversation. Finally, Rex was the veteran GA member who was an old pro at manning the GA telephone hotline. He put me at ease, convincing me that he understood how powerful my urges were. He didn't sugarcoat the realities of our addiction, nor did he try to scare me into abstaining from gambling. He simply informed me that he hit bottom in prison, where he ended up after writing bad checks to cover his gambling debts. "When my wife brought the kids to visit me, that was my wake-up call. The shame I felt motivated me to surrender my addiction to God."

At that point, I was both physically and mentally exhausted. I thanked Rex for being there when I desperately needed him. I ended our conversation by saying, "I'm glad I made it through one day at a time."

"Amen to that," Rex replied. "And by the way, happy anniversary, Bill. You have officially made ninety days in the program!"

"Thanks, Rex. Wow, ninety days without placing a bet. I can't believe I did it."

I went to bed around one, feeling a bit relieved that I had made it through another day without gambling. I was looking forward to receiving my ninety-day key chain at the next meeting.

At about three thirty, I woke up drenched in sweat and shaking. My urge to gamble left my entire body feeling like one gigantic mosquito bite, and no amount of willpower would have been able to stop me from scratching myself. For some strange reason, I felt abandoned. I became overwhelmed with sadness, and I started crying. I hated feeling this way and knew I had to do something, anything, to get a grip on myself. My body was experiencing something akin to drug withdrawal. I had technically reached ninety days of abstinence, but I felt like a rubber band that had simply been pulled back, waiting to snap. And snap I did. It's as if my addiction was taunting me for reaching a milestone, screaming, "Big deal, you ain't shit!"

After throwing on some clothes, I drove to a card club about forty minutes away. My bank had a branch directly across from the club's main entrance, so I stopped there, and with my gold ATM card, I was able to withdraw $500 from my checking account. It seemed like it took forever for the machine to dispense the twenty-five twenties into the chute. But as soon as the shuffling sound stopped, I pushed open the metal cover, grabbed the money along with my card and receipt, and dashed into the club so I could get my fix.

By the time the sun rose, the $500 was gone, along with $1,000 in cash advances I took out from my credit card. So that's how I celebrated my ninety-day birthday—by going on a gambling binge, which would continue for about a month. I never received my ninety-day key chain. No one in GA brought it up, and I didn't think I deserved it.

At the next meeting, I stated during my "share" that I learned something important about myself: I cannot work my recovery one day at a time. Instead, I have to approach it one second at a time. Otherwise, I let my guard down and succumb to my urges, which were now eating at me every waking minute of the day (as well as in my dreams). When I relapsed on my ninety-day birthday, it was like the floodgates of my addiction had opened up, and I was making up for lost time.

THIRTEEN

FALLEN HERO

In early August 1987, I received a call from Paula Gilmore, an acquaintance who was working for ESL, a defense contractor in Sunnyvale, California, in the heart of Silicon Valley. They desperately needed a corporate employment manager, and Paula was trying to recruit me for the job. I told her I was flattered, but I was pursuing my dream of working for myself. Besides, it was highly unlikely that my clients would let me off the hook. Paula indicated that she understood my position but thought it would be a good idea for me to meet her boss to discuss how I could assist their organization as a consultant.

When I met with Paula and a woman named Terri Roberts, the director of human relations, over lunch, all they kept talking about was how perfect I was for the full-time position. I actually became agitated with them and expressed my displeasure at being invited there under false pretenses. I informed them that under no circumstances would I consider the job. I just wasn't interested and didn't feel that I could trust Terri as a boss. They backed off and assured me that they would respect my wishes.

As we were finishing coffee and dessert, Paula excused herself to powder her nose, leaving Terri and me to banter away in small talk. Out of the blue, she mentioned our common backgrounds studying psychology in college and asked if I ever had any regrets not pursuing it as a career. I informed Terri that I did work as a crisis counselor for a short period after receiving my degree and enjoyed it, but the notorious low pay in community mental health pushed me back to the private sector.

"Did you find that experience helpful in the corporate setting?"

"People ask me that all the time," I replied. "I joke that I used to work with patients who were heavily medicated and, in my opinion, some of them didn't need to be; and now, I work with executives who aren't medicated . . . and many of them should be."

Terri burst into laughter, causing nearby diners to gawk at us. "I love it!" she exclaimed.

I continued, "It's amazing how a background in crisis counseling comes in handy when dealing with difficult people and stressful situations in the business environment. I mean, in human resources, we're constantly putting out fires."

Terri nodded strongly in agreement. She stored tidbits of this discussion in her brain. Six months later, she would retrieve it and put it to use.

In early September, I was home recovering from oral surgery. The endodontist's orders were to rest at home and avoid talking. The swelling and intermittent bleeding kept me sidelined, so he really didn't have anything to be concerned about. He prescribed pain medication containing codeine, but I never touched it. I've always been adverse to taking medicine, partially because of fears of becoming dependent on painkillers, so I just toughed it out.

There have actually been occasions when I've felt so helpless battling my gambling urges that I thought about intentionally switching to another addiction, such as alcohol. But the truth is that nothing else ever numbed my emotional pain and eased my anxieties as effectively as sitting at a blackjack table or day-trading in the stock market.

One afternoon during my recovery, I awoke from a nap with a strange vision. At first, I shrugged it off as a bad dream, but it kept hounding me. Then I realized that it was something that I had experienced before. Beginning at age four when I lay near death in the hospital, I would sometimes experience something strange, yet reassuring, and acknowledging it would end up having life-and-death consequences throughout my lifetime. Some might regard it as a sixth sense and others as a premonition, but I had learned to accept it as spiritual guidance. This "gift" kept me alive on the streets, and now it was telling me that my presence was needed at ESL.

I spent the remainder of Labor Day weekend arguing with myself. Part of me felt that it was a crazy idea and not worth jeopardizing my current projects, not to mention damaging my credibility. My intuitive voice, on the other hand, was telling me that I needed to let fate run its course. I reminded myself to approach this issue in the same manner as my recovery, which is to take things a moment at a time. I knew that there was nothing I could do until Tuesday. Realistically, it had been nearly a month since I'd met with Terri—who was anxious to fill the position—so odds were the job was no longer available.

Terri was pleasantly surprised to hear from me after Labor Day. She informed me that they were about to make a job offer to the backup candidate, but she said the job was mine if I wanted it. We agreed to meet the following afternoon to discuss the specifics, including my salary.

One benefit that I saw for taking the job had to do with my gambling. I had been struggling unsuccessfully to stay clean. I was actually breaking even in wins and losses lately, but the fact that I couldn't control my urges was an ongoing concern. My hope was that having the structure of a regular job would keep me out of trouble, at least for the time being.

Terri understood that I had obligations to my clients that I needed to fulfill even if I signed on. The bigger question was whether my clients would go along with the idea. I informed Terri that if any of my clients balked, I would be forced to pass on the job. In her Pollyanna tone of voice, Terri grinned and said, "I know it's all going to work out. You just wait and see . . ."

One by one, I contacted my clients. ICD didn't have any problems with it. In fact, they were ecstatic that I would be working in a different industry, which meant they wouldn't have to worry about me recruiting my former co-workers. They would also be released from paying my quarterly consulting fee. Surprisingly, my other three clients were understanding and gave their blessings, as long as I didn't compromise my services to them. One factor that provided reassurance to my clients was my promise that my assignment at ESL would last no more than six months. My gut told me that my spiritual mission would be complete within that time frame. I told Terri that I would reassess my role at ESL in six months. She knew that I had a lot of qualms about taking the job. I was committed to giving it my all, but I was in the enviable position of not depending on it for my livelihood.

From the moment I became an ESL employee, I was miserable. When I reported to work Monday morning, I discovered that three members of my staff were out of the office for various reasons. My group was in charge of new-hire orientation, so instead of sitting in as a new employee, I ended up conducting the presentation for about a dozen people. I had researched the company and studied the benefits information thoroughly, so I wasn't completely in the dark. But when someone asked how long I had been with the company, my cover was blown. "Oh great, it's the blind leading the blind," someone whispered.

ESL, a subsidiary of TRW, employed about ten human relations managers, and the majority of them did not want me there. My position had been left vacant for about three years, and the job description had changed considerably. It didn't help matters any that Terri announced to the entire department that I was coming in to clean house. Suffice it to say that a welcoming committee did not greet me, nor did I see a red carpet anywhere. On the contrary, the nonverbal receptions I received were more in the line of *Go away. We don't want you here.*

The reporting structure was complex. I oversaw

the entire employment function, so dotted lines ran between myself and the other managers. But Terri was the director, so we had dotted lines to her as well. If that wasn't enough, the HR managers were accountable to the executives of their respective organizations, so you had more lines running across the chart. A map of the world equipped with laser beams capable of crisscrossing and hitting moving targets would not have been enough to sort out the reporting structure in our department. The one glimmer of hope I had was Amy, a personnel assistant in my department whom I would come to regard as my protégée. Amy was intelligent, results-oriented, and able to maintain her composure under immense pressure.

Accountability, cooperation, and change were my biggest challenges. The only time I felt in control and productive was when I performed work for my external clients.

Soon after I started working at ESL, our parent company instituted drug testing for all new hires and also random testing for employees. Some employees selected for testing refused, submitting their resignation, citing invasion of privacy, while others hailed it as a tool to ensure a more responsible, productive workforce. What intrigued me was the large number of subjects, both applicants and employees, who were taking illegal substances but went ahead and submitted urine samples anyway. A few cried foul when informed of the positive results, threatening to sue both the company and the drug lab, but we never heard from them again. Others admitted their drug problems and stated that they felt invincible, believing that somehow they could beat the test.

I suspected that some of my colleagues wanted to use the drug test to conspire against me. When we were evaluating vendors to perform the drug screening, six of us went to visit one of the labs. Near the end of our tour, Carrie, one of the other HR managers, suggested that all of us undergo the tests. It was common knowledge within the department that I wasn't a Boy Scout growing up. At our next staff meeting, Carrie brought along the test results and asked if anyone had a problem with her openly discussing the findings. A few eyes rolled toward me, but I didn't think much of it. After someone simulated a drum roll by banging their fingers on the conference table, Carrie unsealed the envelope and announced, "Wow, all the tests came back negative . . . even Bill's." When she mentioned my name, a few other managers in the room had bewildered expressions on their faces. I thought to myself, *I'm no druggie. Now, if the test screened for gambling addiction, then you would have nailed me.*

Each week, my therapist and members of GA were subjected to my diatribe about loathing my job. I was barely hanging on without gambling, which would have provided a much-needed escape for me.

Ellen suggested an exercise that helped tremendously. I established a ritual in which I composed a resignation letter every Friday afternoon, articulating all my frustrations and the reasons why the job wasn't right for me. Releasing my troubling thoughts was therapeutic and a way to remind myself that I wasn't there for conventional reasons.

To get through each workday, I integrated what I learned in GA and approached things one minute at a time. Reciting the Serenity Prayer in my head repeatedly was also my saving grace: *God, grant me the serenity to accept the things I cannot change, the courage to change the things I can, and the wisdom to know the difference.* I have to admit, though, that there were times when I took things personally. I began to think that my assignment to work at ESL was simply God's way of punishing me.

Once, I reached a boiling point and actually turned in my resignation to Terri. I became infuriated with her and couldn't take it anymore, spiritual mission or not. It came about during my ninth week at ESL, when I confronted Terri about her lack of support. The other HR managers had undermined virtually all my ideas and efforts, and Terri wasn't doing anything about it.

The resignation letter was short and sweet: I simply gave two weeks' notice, dated it, and signed my name. I sealed it in an envelope, walked over, and placed it on the center of Terri's desk. The drive home that evening was nothing short of liberating. *I am free of that place. There is just no logical reason for me to be there. What a bunch of losers. All they're good for is playing politics and kissing ass.*

I treated myself to a nice dinner at a Japanese restaurant, watched television when I got home, and went to bed feeling relaxed. But my sleep was far from restful. I had a nightmare, and it was extremely violent. I sat up on the bed realizing that my spiritual work at ESL was not complete. I also suspected that gunfire would play a role in it. I sat there pouting and resenting the prophecy. I had no idea that the survival skills I developed from the gang wars and my counseling experience were about to be put to the test.

By the next morning, I knew I couldn't go through with the resignation. I walked into the office feeling depressed, and as soon as Terri's assistant saw me, she picked up the telephone and alerted her.

Within a minute, Terri walked into my office, closed the door, and gave me another trite pep talk.

"Bill, I know you're a true professional and not a quitter. There are things going on at a higher level that I can't share with you, but you need to keep the faith. You may not think so, but you're already making a difference. I'm just sorry that there are a number of other crises that need my attention as well."

I sat there and just nodded my head. What irked me was Terri leaving my office convinced that she had sweet-talked me into rescinding my resignation. I could hardly stand the idea that I was giving her that satisfaction.

On Tuesday, February 16, 1988, I was driving to work and just knew something big was going to happen that day. Heck, I was about five months into my job at ESL, and with all the vibes I had been experiencing lately with violent undertones, something just had to be up in the spiritual sense. The closer I got to the office, the more anxious, scared, and also curious I became. I had a lot of catching up to do on paperwork, so I had kept my calendar cleared except for one interview. The Information Technology hiring manager that I set up the interview for preferred midafternoon appointments, so I had asked the candidate, Harry Bowlin, to come in at three o'clock. That decision still haunts me today.

I had never heard the name Richard Farley before, but he was an ESL employee with a top-secret clearance who had become obsessed with a young, attractive co-worker named Laura Black. Eventually, he was fired for harassing her. This all happened before my time at ESL.

Harry Bowlin had his own obsessions. He hated being late, so he arrived at 2:45 in the north parking lot of building M5, a two-story structure that housed approximately 225 ESL employees. After pulling into a space and shutting off his engine, Harry found himself looking across at a burly man sitting in an RV. The man gave Harry the creeps; he was wearing a headband, appeared agitated, and had an empty stare in his eyes. It was Richard Farley, disgruntled employee and soon-to-be mass murderer. He had returned to take on the entire company and was carrying enough firepower to achieve his goal. The arsenal that Farley was lugging included three handguns, two shotguns, a high-powered automatic rifle, and bandoliers of ammunition. He was also wearing a shooting vest stocked with bullet shells, one hand was gloved, and he was wearing earplugs and carrying a buck knife. Farley didn't step out of his RV until Harry got out of his car and was out of sight. He couldn't risk drawing attention to himself. It was critical for Farley to approach and enter M5 as inconspicuously as possible.

After being alerted that my candidate had arrived, I called the hiring manager, but he was away from his desk. So I stepped out and walked the twenty or so paces from my office to the lobby door, opened it, and greeted Harry. I took him back to my office, and just as we sat down, the phone rang. Of course, it was the hiring manager letting me know that he was available to meet with Harry. As I was escorting Harry across the lobby to the IT department in the north wing, I heard some commotion above us. I looked up and saw people at the top of the stairwell, frantically running down, some leaping two and three steps at a time.

"Hey, what's going on?" I asked loudly.

"There's a man with a gun in the building," someone shouted.

Then *bang!* A loud blast was heard, which I knew was gunfire. The walls seemed to shake, perhaps from the echo. I literally shoved Harry out the door, and when we were outside, we heard more rounds being discharged from the second floor. Folks were still running out of the building in cowered positions, jerking each time a blast went off.

For a moment, I assumed that my spiritual mission was to keep Harry safe and that my work was done, but that was not the case. It was only the beginning of an eleven-hour drama that would change my life forever.

After realizing that none of my co-workers in the human relations department was outside, I pushed my way back into the building, swung open the lobby door leading to my area, and began screaming at people to leave. The soundproofing was so good that as the door closed behind me, the noise from the lobby was muted again. In order to guard against classified information being overheard, all the offices and conference rooms are noise-insulated. I quickly rehearsed in my head how to warn them without causing a massive stampede.

"There's an emergency! Everyone should leave the building right away! Don't panic, but get out as quickly as possible!" I repeated this over and over.

At the time, thirty to thirty-five of my colleagues were in our office wing, and about half heeded my warning right away; the others needed more prodding. I ran up and down the hall, yelling into offices, opening and banging on doors, using my arms to point directly at people at a distance, waving them toward the exit. Two people were on the phone and didn't seem to understand the gravity of the situation, so I yanked the receivers from their hands and gave them a nudge. Gina, our temp, walked toward me, seeking an explanation, but I held my palm out and screamed, "No, just go!" Twice, I looked toward the exit to gauge the progress of the evacuation, and each time, the doorway to the lobby seemed narrower, especially when two people were trying to squeeze through at the same time. The crisis was creating funny illusions.

Just as I dashed out through the double doors of our building for the second time in less than ten minutes, more gunfire could be heard. My co-workers, including those who questioned my bizarre behavior, put two and two together and realized that we were in a war zone. Most of them started running as fast as they could. One woman in a skirt took off her white high heels and sprinted past a heavyset man who was barreling along huffing and puffing, as though he were standing still. Thank God nobody fell and got trampled. In my estimate, there were close to seventy-five people clustered together, running for their lives.

After the area was vacated, the gunman fired a shot from the top of the stairs into the human relations area. From his vantage point, he had a clear view of the entrance to our department. The bullet from his rifle shattered the wall of glass that separated the lobby and our department—ricocheting in front of my office where I often stood. I noticed it the day after the massacre, and the deep hole in the carpet is embedded in my memory.

We heard sirens and about ten police cars arrived almost all at the same time, with lights flashing and tires screeching. A couple of them stopped at the north and south intersections to close off the road. Half a dozen stopped in front of our building in the middle of the street, while others pulled into the driveways. Most of the M5 employees naturally headed toward M3, the neighboring building, away from the gunfire. I kept walking until I reached M1, the next building over, where the executive offices were located. I felt safer knowing that a huge structure stood between the gunman and me.

I didn't know it at the time, but two people in my department did not make it out. One was a peer, Ruth, whose office was located two doors down from mine. She was in a closed-door meeting with an engineering manager from M3. Ruth told me later that she didn't hear a thing, but I swore that I banged on her door when I was rushing through and warning everyone. The second person left behind was Amy from my group.

Amy was in a conference room with eight other women, where a baby shower was being thrown for Kelly, a co-worker. By the time they heard gunshots, most of the employees in the building had already escaped. When Amy's group reached the lobby, the front door was closed and locked. Due to security measures, the only way to unlock the door is by pressing a buzzer located at the receptionist's desk. So Amy ran around and activated the buzzer so others could escape. As Amy watched the last person run out, she yelled for her co-worker Kim to wait and hold the door open, but it was too late—Kim dashed out in a panic and never looked back, leaving Amy to fend for herself. Amy heard more blasts, so she retreated to our department and hid under a desk in one of the private offices, with Farley standing at the top of the lobby stairs just above her. At one point, Amy dialed the security department and notified them of her whereabouts, but the rookie officer on the line did not take Amy seriously and told her not to be a nuisance and to calm down by putting her head between her knees. He assured her that he would call her right back, but he never did.

All of this was recorded, and the young security officer would be reprimanded in the weeks ahead.

Nearly an hour later, Amy was tired of feeling like a sitting duck, so she crawled on her belly along the corridor to the back exit, eventually making it out the south side of the building. As Amy knelt inside the glass door, she saw a SWAT member across the way behind a car. Amy waved him to come get her. He motioned her to run to him. She was afraid to move. Amy waved again. He wouldn't budge. He signaled for her to come. They were having their own standoff. *The policeman's armed and wearing a bulletproof vest. Why can't he come and get me?* she wondered. Finally, she crouched down and ran. As soon as she reached him, they both huddled and he led her safely from the parking lot by running in a zigzag pattern.

Believing that my work was done, I sat outside the executive offices in M1 and observed all the chaos going on around me. I felt generally calm and was making mental notes of the different ways people were reacting to the crisis. Many were in shock—some speechless—but most were screaming, crying, and shaking uncontrollably. A few stepped up and took charge, including Bob Kohler, ESL's president;

Lew Franklin, a vice president; and lo and behold, my boss, Terri Roberts. Bob and Lew seemed to know what needed to be done and went right to it. Terri threw herself into the fray and did what she does best—which is to delegate.

Things seemed to have reached a crescendo at around four thirty. The executive area, aka "mahogany row," of M1 had been designated as the command center. Police commanders and investigators were scurrying around, trying to gather statements from witnesses, while a hostage negotiator was trying to establish contact with the gunman. Simultaneously, half a dozen crisis counselors from a local hospital had arrived and were playing musical chairs, tending to traumatized employees whose line formation for each therapist was running ten deep and multiplying. Counselors listened to umpteen versions of what had happened in M5, held employees while they cried, reassured them that they were now safe, and advocated breathing techniques for relaxation as though they were Lamaze coaches. Many employees who claimed that they were okay and wanted to leave were told to wait until friends or family members could pick them up.

While all this was going on, dozens of family members of employees heard the news reports and were converging around the reception desk in the lobby demanding information about loved ones who were unaccounted for. Camera crews were broadcasting all of this live to the nation.

I was holding Sean, Kelly's newborn son, when someone alerted me that a woman was trying to get my attention. I looked up and saw Terri motioning to me. I passed Sean back to Kelly and went to find out what was on Terri's mind.

"We need you to get involved, Bill. We've got to get organized. We're getting conflicting information about what's going on inside M5. We've got people trapped in there, and we know at least one person is dead. Whatever you can do, Bill—and grab whomever you can to help you."

Terri, who was already in M1 when the crisis began, proceeded to introduce me to a police commander and a lieutenant who ended up being my counterparts for the better part of the next ten hours. I met with the supervising therapist, and we developed a rating system so that all employees requiring treatment would be referred to her staff based on severity of their emotional crisis. Granted, some individuals demanding immediate attention were put off, while others who swore they were fine (but obviously in denial) got moved to the front of the line. Many employees were in shock and reacted by detaching themselves from the situation. They didn't know where they were and had blank stares in their eyes. My previous experience at San Francisco

General Hospital's Psychiatric Emergency Services and subsequent work with psychotics in an outpatient facility was all coming back to me.

We needed to do something about the family members showing up in the lobby. It was decided that I would be in charge of screening them, writing down names of everyone working in M5 who was reported missing. The list I had was cross-referenced with the information from witnesses and the police. It was decided that the executive conference room would be used as the family support center. Family members of employees who were confirmed trapped or injured were directed there. The bond that family members established proved to be very comforting. Strangers were becoming kindred souls almost immediately, holding hands and even praying together. They did a better job supporting one another than any of us could have done. I found it difficult to be in there. It was too emotional for me. I had to stay objective and focused—for them as well as for their loved ones.

With help from members of my staff, I created a telephone hotline for friends and family of missing employees. This allowed telephone operators manning the company switchboard to route select calls directly into our command center. Some loved ones had received phone calls from workers hiding in the building and passed the information on to us. Others were calling from across the country, desperately seeking reassurance that their sons, daughters, mothers, and fathers were alive and well. Some made the mistake of contacting the media, which became a real nuisance.

Members of the media called into the hotline claiming to be relatives of employees to get access to company officials and information about the drama unfolding. Worst of all, when they gained access to information regarding the location of employees trapped inside M5, they broadcast it over the airwaves, jeopardizing lives. The gunman had access to a radio, and when we went in later that night, it was turned on to the news station that was leaking out the locations. Staying a step ahead of the media, as well as the gunman, ended up being my most challenging task.

In the midst of a crisis, people's instincts and senses can become extremely sharp, much like animals surviving in the wild. It didn't take long for relatives to sense that I had specific information regarding their loved ones. I avoided eye contact and communication with family members, but they hunted me down and tried to get a sense of how good or bad things were based on my body language. A few screamed at me and had to be escorted away. I didn't blame them. The fate of so many was out of our hands.

Just before seven o'clock, I turned one of my lists over to Lieutenant John Griffin. It contained the exact locations of a dozen employees hiding on the first floor of M5, including my colleague Ruth. She had not moved from her office since the drama began. Kevin Galloway, the manager she had been in a meeting with, was a hero in his own right. Hours earlier, Kevin had crawled out, taking the same route as Amy, ending up at the rear exit. But as police officers gave him the thumbs up to run out, Kevin turned around and retreated to Ruth's office. Kevin had given her his word that he would not abandon her, and he kept his promise. Kevin tried to convince Ruth to crawl out with him, but she was too frightened, so they stayed put. SWAT team members eventually rescued them, along with ten others, at about seven thirty. According to my list, we still had twenty-four employees unaccounted for on the second floor. Most were engineers.

Shortly thereafter, we received news that three employees, including Laura Black, the object of Farley's obsession, were being treated for gunshot wounds at various hospitals. Farley had found Laura in her office and shot her in the left shoulder. The shotgun blast collapsed her lung. But even as Laura lay on the ground bleeding profusely, she managed to kick the door shut on Farley, who moved on. He would later ask the negotiator if Laura was alive. It was important for him that she live, "so she could regret all of this."

Around eight thirty, the hostage negotiator convinced Farley to surrender, enticing him with a sandwich and soda. The strategy to wear Farley down apparently worked. When the negotiator notified him that the ice in the soda was melting, that was enough to get Farley out of the building. By nine thirty, the building had been completely swept through by police, who rescued sixteen employees hiding under desks and in the ceiling. It would take another forty-eight hours for us to confirm that the remaining eight missing employees were alive. Not alive and well, but just alive. One programmer analyst, who had found himself face to face with the gunman shortly after he blasted his way into the building, tripped over his co-worker's dead body, the first victim shot by Farley, as he ran through the parking lot. The shocked programmer jumped in his car and headed south, driving nonstop for two hours until he reached his sister's house in Carmel.

Two hours later, Lieutenant Griffin pulled me aside and asked to review my list of missing employees again. Next he proceeded to give me the shocking news:

"Bill, we have seven confirmed dead." After a pause to compose himself, he continued, "There's a problem—we're having trouble identifying some of the bodies, due to massive injuries."

"Well, what about their ID badges?" I asked.

"Some of the badges were blown to bits and there were no other identifications on them," replied the lieutenant.

My only response was, "Shit."

I had been holding myself together throughout the ordeal, suppressing my emotions, functioning much like a robot. But it was finally catching up with me. As I passed the executive conference room, I began to shake, knowing that there was no hope for the remaining family members. I slipped out and found a quiet spot down the hallway, leaned my head back against the wall, and softly recited the Serenity Prayer over and over again. I'm not sure how much it helped, but I was able to keep a poker face and outright lie to individuals who I knew had suddenly become widows, widowers, orphans, and parents of murdered children.

You would think, with all the homicides I lived through from the Chinatown gang wars, that I would be desensitized to what was occurring, but we were in Silicon Valley, the last place I expected to contend with individuals being blown to bits. In many ways, this was more traumatic because I was interfacing directly with the victims' families.

Lieutenant Griffin and the police commander made it clear to Bob, Lew, Terri, and me that we were not to say a word to the relatives regarding the deceased. The coroner still had to make positive IDs on the bodies, and there was protocol to follow in notifying the next of kin. We needed to get into each of the murder victim's personnel files to ascertain whom they stipulated to be notified in an emergency. We couldn't assume just because a relative showed up and expressed concern that he or she was the appropriate person to contact.

One of those waiting to receive official word was Joanne Silverman. She was separated from her husband, Joe, who worked for us on the second floor of M5. Joanne had been pacing back and forth for over six hours, clutching her purse like a security blanket and wearing a long coat buttoned from top to bottom. She reminded me of Bernice, Detective Fish's wife on the television show *Barney Miller*. I knew that Joanne was growing more impatient, and her intuition was telling her that I was withholding information on Joe.

After helping to retrieve the personnel files from our office, I was strolling along mahogany row and noticed Joanne making a beeline for me. The closer she got, the more crazed she looked. I knew what was coming and just let it happen. Part of me believed I deserved it, that I was the bad guy. Joanne grabbed the lapels of my blue pinstriped suit jacket and shook me, yelling, "You know what happened and you're not telling me. What kind of man are you?" Within seconds, she was pulled away from me. Lew walked over and put his arm around me.

"Are you okay, Bill?"

"Yeah, I'll be fine," I replied, as my eyes welled up. Right then, I wanted to tear up my notepad, throw the remnants into the trash can, and just run out of there. I wanted to be in Tahoe so bad I could smell the casinos. There, I could lose myself on the blackjack table. I'd just sit on the stool chair, and the only thing expected of me would be to count to twenty-one over and over again. There would be no guns, no hostages, no dead bodies, no grieving family members—and most of all, no stupid heroes.

Bob successfully negotiated with the police to notify the family members himself. He, Lew, and Terri carried this out between two and three o'clock in the morning. As for me, I stepped into a cab just after two for the long ride home. The police had taped off the parking lot for investigative purposes, so we didn't have access to our vehicles.

Over the next four weeks, I was buried in expediting life insurance claims, providing grief counseling to family members mostly by just being there for them and letting them bend my ears, securing travel arrangements and accommodations for the relatives coming in from around the country (including Laura Black's family), attending funeral services, responding to community assistance, and just putting out umpteen fires.

Many occurrences during this time period can

only be described as small miracles. Not only did these miracles validate my sense of purpose there, but for me, they also made a strong case regarding my destiny at birth.

I received a spiritual message to assist one of the widows. It came as I was driving back to ESL the morning following the massacre. One of the murder victims, Buddy Wilson, was asking me to keep an eye on his wife, Lauren. I had never met him, so it didn't make sense to me, but the way things had been unfolding over the past sixteen hours, I knew that following my intuition was the best course of action. As I got to know Lauren and Buddy's relatives, we discovered many similarities between our families. For example, my son shares a first, middle, and nickname with Buddy and his younger brother (although not in the same order).

Almost immediately after we met, Lauren sensed that I was receiving spiritual guidance from her husband, and she confronted me about it. I had little choice but to own up to feeling his spirit. A personal notebook of Buddy's also appeared out of thin air for Lauren to find, providing her with strength and a much needed connection.

The kindness and generosity from the community were heartwarming. A couple in nearby Los Gatos, who owned a small hotel and were active in local politics, offered to put up all the relatives at no charge. Their offer extended to relatives who lived in town. They were aware that some local family members would not want to return to their homes right away for numerous reasons.

We found out from relatives staying at the hotel that the host couple even went as far as renting limousines so our guests would have transportation whenever they wanted, and they offered to pick up meals for the families in case they wanted to stay in. The couple covered all the expenses and never said a word about remuneration. I only found out about their generosity when the families expressed their gratitude to me, assuming that the company was behind the hospitality and paying for it. The only stipulation the couple had was that their involvement be kept confidential from the public. I made sure Terri, Bob, and Lew knew about this, and from that day forward, ESL made a point of giving the hotel as much business as it could handle.

I also received a message from the owner of a cemetery located in the Peninsula, just north of Silicon Valley. When I returned the call and spoke with the proprietor, he offered to donate plots for the victims. The only condition was that he wanted to remain anonymous.

Then you had the unsavory types. One limousine company offered their services, but wanted to issue a press release announcing their donation to

ESL's victims and their families. The transportation was restricted to remote areas of the city, and only during early morning or late night hours. The added condition was that their service would only be one-way. Essentially, the limo company was offering to strand our families at isolated destinations in the middle of the night. We also received telephone calls offering thousands of dollars to benefit the victims' families. I followed up to verify the donations, only to discover that many were pranks. Some of the victims' families were contacted directly by these people and subjected to their cruel hoaxes.

Nine days after the massacre, the company held a memorial service for the victims. It was standing room only, as more than two thousand people were in attendance. The media was also there in full force. I served as host to both Laura Black's and Buddy Wilson's families. Laura was still recovering from her wounds at Stanford Hospital.

On March 9, I submitted my resignation to Terri, and my last day at ESL was almost six months to the day from when I started. Terri was very gracious and kept repeating, "Bill, I don't know what I would have done without you." It was getting uncomfortable hearing her say it because each time she would be on the verge of breaking down and crying.

We both agreed that my presence there wasn't about the job. My co-workers in the department also made it known that my actions in running back in to alert them of the crisis were nothing short of heroic. I think I was more concerned with having to live with myself if I didn't warn them.

I was never officially recognized for my efforts relating to the massacre, but neither was Amy for saving the group attending the baby shower, nor Kevin Galloway for standing by Ruth during the entire ordeal, nor other employees who risked their lives to help co-workers. One manager received an award for his performance associated with the tragedy, but he wasn't even at work the day of the massacre. His name didn't ring a bell with me. I didn't know if the accolades bestowed on him were politically motivated or if they had to do with accomplishments following the crisis, but it did leave a bad taste in my mouth.

I returned to my consulting practice, but things were far from hunky-dory. I began suffering recurring nightmares about the massacre, complete with Farley chasing me throughout M5. My nightmares weren't limited to ESL; much of the violence I experienced growing up in Chinatown returned to haunt me as well.

I also started second-guessing myself about Harry Bowlin. If I hadn't scheduled his interview for three o'clock that dreadful day, Farley in all likelihood would have entered the building at least ten minutes earlier. Perhaps fewer people would have died—perhaps more. We'll never know, but I just wouldn't let myself off the hook.

As miserable as I was at ESL prior to the massacre, I did not place a single bet during my employment there. I maintained my abstinence and accumulated six months of clean time. I had no explanation for it, except that I believed I had hit bottom and was attending GA meetings regularly and working my recovery program. But that was not the case, as I would discover soon enough. I wasn't even close to hitting the bottom of my barrel.

Financially, I was in very good shape at that point. If you take away my addiction, I'm actually quite resourceful in earning and saving money. I still had most of the original $20,000 in retainers from clients when I launched my business, additional consulting fees, and my salary from ESL. All told, I had almost $40,000 in savings, which meant I could do some serious damage to myself if I relapsed, which is exactly what happened.

Within two weeks after I left ESL, I started gambling again. I justified it by telling myself that God owed me big-time for the six months of hard labor and for my efforts during and after the massacre. It sounds ridiculous now, but that's what I truly believed at the time. On some level, though, I suspected—but didn't want to admit—that the massacre had unleashed all my past demons. The truth is that I wasn't as strong and brave as I appeared during the crisis. Even Lieutenant Griffin commended me for keeping a level head and being able to multitask during the crisis, but I just dissociated from my feelings, which is something I learned to do beginning as a little boy. When I witnessed my first shooting at age eight, I had already been telling myself that only wimps get scared and that fear was a sign of weakness. I got good at keeping it bottled up deep inside. Sometimes I just pretended I was somewhere else. But now all the emotions were stirring up inside of me and spilling out. I didn't have the basic skills or sense of self-worth to deal with it, and gambling provided a temporary relief. It's an unhealthy choice to say the least, but it's something that I had relied on to help me cope—virtually my entire life.

FOURTEEN

VIVA LAS VEGAS

After relapsing following the massacre, I thought it'd be a good idea to get a new GA sponsor. I never did more than exchange pleasantries with Tim at meetings, and I knew I needed more than that; I just wasn't sure how much more. In comparison, other members talked casually about having daily contact with their sponsors, some maintaining dialogue throughout the day and receiving guidance on virtually every aspect of their lives. A few in the program went as far as turning their paychecks over to their sponsors and getting a weekly allowance in the process. They swore that it was the only way for them to pay their bills, honor their debts, and stay out of trouble. Fine for them, but I wasn't about to let anyone touch a dime of my money, and having a sponsor check up on me every single day seemed like overkill. In hindsight, giving up control of my finances and having a strong mentor and support system were exactly what I needed.

I blamed myself for selecting a hands-off sponsor, but I didn't think Tim would be so aloof. He was secretary of the meeting and seemed to have a strong persona. I often wondered if he was sponsoring anyone else and, if so, what type of relationship they had. I'm pretty sure it wasn't just me. I don't recall anyone having a phone conversation with Tim, so I didn't take it personally. Fred, my new sponsor, was only a slight improvement. He never initiated contact, but at least he returned my calls.

Essentially, the battle waged on inside me between good and evil. There was Bill L., who desperately wanted to stop gambling and to seek guidance from GA, engaging in a brutal struggle with William, the frightened child who felt worthless and didn't trust anyone, including himself. At this point, William, who was more resourceful and learned to escape his troubles by gambling, had the upper hand.

I started patronizing local card clubs and playing a game called pai gow poker, which is a loose variation of pai gow, the Chinese tile game. The latter is widely known as a game for high rollers and is the original version of baccarat. I only recall my father playing pai gow on special occasions, for instance, during Chinese New Year celebrations, and each time he got taken to the cleaners. I'm pretty sure that pai gow was the game my biological, paternal grandfather was addicted to in southern China. If this were the case, I would think that my father would have been turned off by the game, unless he was subconsciously punishing himself. I have personally seen players in card rooms bet the title to their houses in a single hand. It was insane, with players on the losing end screaming bloody murder. Winners were accused of switching the tiles, of colluding with other players, and of conspiring with dealers. With so much money at stake, I suspect that there was some truth to the accusations. I wondered if much fuss was made when my father was being placed as a wager in some dirty hut in China.

Pai gow poker, on the other hand, is straightforward: Players are dealt seven cards, from which two hands of poker are formed; the top hand consists of two cards, and the bottom and stronger hand consists of five cards.

I had signed on a new client, who ended up occupying most of my time and who required me to work on-site. Unfortunately, their headquarters in the East Bay were conveniently located within ten minutes of the two card rooms I frequented. At times I'd gamble all night and report back to my client's office dressed in the same clothes that I'd worn the previous day. When I got funny looks, I tried to portray myself as a Don Juan with a stable of girlfriends in the vicinity, but the only affair I was carrying on involved ladies (queens) on a deck of cards.

One day, I received a telegram from my bank notifying me that my ATM card had been deactivated due to suspicious activity on my account. When I called to inquire about the problem, the supervisor informed me that someone had been using my card to withdraw the daily maximum amount of $500 just before midnight—then taking out another $500 shortly after midnight. Although the transactions occurred within a few minutes of one another, they were posted on two separate days. The activity was inconsistent with my history, and it pointed to someone who intentionally wanted to withdraw as much cash as possible in the shortest time allowed. So far, $4,000 had been removed from my account within a ten-day period in this manner. Instead of being grateful for the bank's concern, I told the supervisor to mind her own business and demanded that she reactivate the ATM card as soon as possible. She obviously wasn't aware that one of the worse things anyone can do is to get in the way of an addict and his drug of choice.

By July 1988, I was spending all my spare time in the card clubs, feeling compelled to escape, but I had no idea from what. I was getting tired of leading a double life, and one evening in the club's restroom, out of desperation, I prayed to Buddy Wilson and the other victims of ESL. *Listen, folks, I don't know why things turned out the way they did. For some reason, I'm still here and you're there. I did my best to help your families get through this, and right now I need you. Please help me win. I just need one big win and I'll stop . . . please.*

I didn't get the big win, but something else happened: I stopped gambling—abruptly following the prayer. One of the reasons had to do with Asian gang members who were working in one of the clubs. These guys had ties to Triads in Asia. I became friendly with them and saw that I was falling back into my old pattern. I reminded myself that I was lucky to get out alive once; getting involved with the underworld again would be tantamount to gambling with my life. Shortly after I stopped hanging around the card club that employed the gang members, federal agents raided the establishment. Subsequently, both the management and employees were charged with money laundering, loan sharking, drug trafficking, and murder. Perhaps my spiritual friends answered my prayers in the manner that they saw fit. I escaped physical harm and my record remained clean. I did not take this lightly; I knew that my gambling almost led me into a black hole, and this knowledge jolted me enough to abstain for the time being.

✳

By June 1989, I had amassed eleven straight months of clean time and was looking forward to celebrating my one-year anniversary the following month, complete with a dinner party and pinning ceremony. I seemed to be taking to the program, no longer questioning the merits of the Combo Book or passing judgment on the behavior of other members. But at the same time, I was keeping my distance. When asked to help set up the room, make coffee, or serve as one of the trusted servants (such as secretary), I always had an excuse for not being available. In most instances, I hid behind my career, stating that I was too busy with my clients and was lucky just to be able to attend meetings. There's no doubt in my mind that if I had been more involved in the program, I would have had my one-year anniversary.

I was consulting full time with a client in San Jose who was developing computer-aided design technology. My primary responsibility was assisting the company with their recruiting efforts, but they were fully aware of my background in competitive analyses.

I was commuting to my client's headquarters

three times a week and working out of my home the other two days. One morning, the manager of human resources called me at home. The request she made left me pale as a ghost and speechless.

"Bill, the annual Design Automation Conference is coming up at the end of the month, and our divisional vice president would like you to attend, specifically to gather intelligence on our competitors."

"Okay, Diane, sure. What are the exact dates and location?"

"Let's see . . . I have the registration form right here. Here it is . . . exhibition area opens on Sunday, June 25, and the conference closes on Thursday, June 29. We'd like you there for the entire period and would like you to submit a report by the following Monday."

"All right, and the location?"

"Oh yes, it's in Las Vegas. We're taking care of the travel arrangements, and I'll let you know in the next few days what your itinerary looks like. I assume you'll want to fly out of SFO. I'll also have a list of companies and topics we'd like you to focus on. Do you have any questions?"

After I heard the words "Las Vegas," everything else sounded muffled and distant. I felt as if I had just been swept off my feet and thrown into a freezing pond.

"Bill, are you there?"

"Um . . . yes, I'm here."

"So do you have any questions?"

"No, not right now."

I got ahold of Fred right away, and he said it was a bad idea to spend any time in Vegas. Later that evening at my home meeting, I received a lot of support for the predicament I was in. Everyone was concerned about the temptation of being in the gambling mecca of the world. Even members of the GA Mafia cautioned me. More than one member pointed out the directive on page 17 of the Combo Book that states "Don't go in or near gambling establishments." The input I received ranged from using my son as an excuse for not being able to travel to coming clean about my addiction, in hopes that Diane would be sympathetic and supportive of my recovery. But I didn't really consider Diane a friend, and I couldn't take a chance that my addiction would not hurt my reputation, so being open about it wasn't a viable option.

I thought long and hard, rehearsing various dialogues in my head, but when I spoke with Diane again, my attempt to get a waiver from the assignment came out all wrong.

"You see, Diane, I have strong beliefs against gambling, and I don't have any desire to be in Vegas."

"Bill, we're not asking you to do anything unusual. You presented yourself as someone who would be willing to help us with recruiting as well as competitive analyses. We don't think it's unreasonable for you to attend this conference, wherever it's held. If you think about it, Las Vegas isn't that far away. It's not like we're asking you to travel to the East Coast or out of the country."

So that's how we left it. Diane had no clue regarding the real reason I didn't want to step foot in the desert. If I quit my assignment, it would have severely damaged my reputation. I also didn't want to be known as a quitter. The fact that I was acting stubborn didn't bode well for my recovery. I started trying to convince myself that I could handle it, that I was stronger than my addiction. In other words, my damn ego was rearing its ugly head.

My brothers and sisters in the fellowship offered their support nonetheless. They continually emphasized the need for me to attend GA meetings while I was in Vegas and to stay in close contact with the local members there as well as from home.

Someone in GA mentioned that there was a hotel in Vegas that didn't have a casino on its premises. That sounded too good to be true. I found out that it was the St. Tropez, and they promote themselves as the nongaming resort of Las Vegas. When I inquired about their room availability, I discovered that the hotel is in such great demand that they're booked six months in advance. I was out of luck.

There was one thing I needed to take care of before attending DAC (Design Automation Conference). My trusty old Datsun 310 GX needed to be put out to pasture. I had logged over 250,000 miles on the original engine, and it was starting to fall apart. I ended up donating it to the National Kidney Foundation.

I dropped the car off, signed over the pink slip, and arrived at the bus stop shortly after one o'clock. It was a warm, sunny day. Out of nowhere, an elderly woman walked up to me and started ranting about something. It took a minute for me to figure out that she was upset because she assumed I was enrolled at the high school up the street and was cutting classes. I was approaching my thirty-fifth birthday, so it was quite flattering. Of course, my worst gambling lay ahead, and it would age me mercilessly. My guess is that seven years later, if that same woman encountered me, she would think that I'd wandered off from some convalescent home.

With nearly a year of clean time, I had plenty of money saved up, so it was easy for me to pay cash to purchase my next car, a 1989 Acura Integra. It was the first new car I had ever owned. Sadly, shortly after returning from Vegas, I would be forced to sell it to the bank.

As we disembarked from the plane on Sunday afternoon, I heard the clanging sound of slot machines even before reaching the gate entrance. The airport even smelled like a casino. It was over a hundred degrees outside. I was feeling nervous and excited at the same time. One thing for sure—my eleven months of abstinence was slipping before my eyes.

By the time I reached the registration desk at the hotel, which wasn't that far from the entrance, I must have passed more than fifty gaming tables and hundreds of slots. In Vegas, it is hard-core gambling, no doubt about it. At least in Lake Tahoe, gambling is mixed in with the aesthetics of the snow-covered mountains, trees, and blue waters. But in Vegas during the late eighties, it was in-your-face wagering and direct sensory overload. Every inch of the hotels seemed to be crammed with either gambling or gamblers—take your pick. I brought along tons of reading material, and my intended strategy for the trip was to head straight to the convention center by bus each day, conduct my business, and head back to the hotel, where I would lock myself in the room. I was going to call one or two GA secretaries out there and make arrangements to attend their meetings.

Late Sunday afternoon, I spent a couple of hours at the exhibition hall, and it was time well spent. Most of my client's competitors were still setting up, which was an ideal opportunity for me to catch them with their guard down. An ID badge with the name Scott Guyton had been left for me at the hotel by one of my client's employees. I used it to gain access into the area, but purposely removed it after I entered. Attendees were required to wear their badges at all times, but I didn't have any problems circulating around incognito. Part of my modus operandi was to appear authoritative, even around the security personnel. If people are convinced that they're supposed to know you, then they don't want to embarrass themselves by questioning your identity. I was fully aware that if my cover were blown, my client would deny any knowledge or involvement with me.

So I made my rounds and did what I do best, which was to get individuals to divulge proprietary information. One technique I use is to ask questions in a way that puts people on the defensive. There really isn't much to it. It just takes a bit of confidence and an unethical mind-set. I approached a booth and introduced myself as Ron Chin, a consultant for a number of start-ups in Silicon Valley who are evaluating CAD programs. I asked them about their products and how they compared with their competitors. Many shared details of products in development, including features above and beyond what other companies were offering. Some didn't hesitate to trash their competitors and shared rumors of quality and performance issues. I collected their business cards and moved on to my next target, armed with information that would be used for "networking."

"So-and-so company is about to release a product with these enhanced features. What will you offer in comparison? Also, there are rumors that your system has a major flaw; what do you have to say about that?" Sometimes, I was the one making up the rumor, especially when I smelled a rookie manning the booth, who would end up sharing the crown jewels on the company's technology.

I also made sure I got a sense of what's being said about my client in the industry, from competitors as well as end users and prospective customers. Pricing information was critical, as was identifying prospective candidates to recruit. In those situations, Diane or the hiring manager would follow up on the leads I generated to protect my cover.

Speaking of cover, mine was blown, about an hour into my expedition. Brett Fullerton was a vice president whom I had tried to recruit for ICD. I hadn't seen or spoken with him since I ventured off on my own. But as I was making my rounds, Brett spotted me and walked over with one of his managers.

"Whoa! Hey, stranger, fancy seeing you here. I heard you turned into a hired gun. So how are you, Bill?"

"Oh, fine, Brett. It's good to see you."

"Pardon me, Stu, this is Bill Lee, who used to work at ICD. Bill, this is Stu Marshall, our CAD director."

"Wait a minute," replied Stu. "I thought you said your name was Ron when I spoke with you earlier."

Brett started chuckling and said, "I'll explain later. Stu, why don't you let me catch up with you in a few minutes? I need to ask Bill something." After Stu walked off with a puzzled look, Brett was still grinning.

"So whom are you snooping around for these days?"

"Micron Graphics," I replied. "They're taking up most of my time these days."

"Well now, is there any way of getting my hands on some of that juicy data you're collecting?"

"Sure, just give me a call. We'll compare notes next week." With that, Brett went off to commence *his* intelligence gathering.

Upon returning to my hotel room, I was revved up from my undercover assignment. I was fired up and overflowing with energy. I was proud of what I had accomplished that first day, and I felt unstoppable. I did some stretching exercises, took a shower, and then ordered dinner from room service. It took over an hour for the food to arrive, and in the meantime, I couldn't keep still. All the television channels seemed to be programmed to "how to gamble" infomercials, including blackjack, baccarat, craps, and of course, pai gow poker. I opened my GA Combo Book, but the more I read, the stronger my urges to gamble. I may have been sitting in a quiet room, but the inside of my head was drowning in noises of clanging slot machines, bright lights, images of people on the casino floor, and me sitting at blackjack and pai gow poker tables. Knowing that the action was just steps away from the elevator made it all the more tempting—or shall I say, irresistible? *Stupid me, why did I even come here?*

After dinner, I knelt beside the bed and recited the Serenity Prayer over and over. I thought about calling local GA members and getting myself to a meeting, and I wanted to call Fred, too, but a big part of me felt ashamed and didn't want to appear weak. Looking back, my undercover work had inflated my ego and made it harder for me to reach out for help. Eventually, when I truly began to work my recovery, specifically tackling Step work, I would discover not only that it wasn't wise for me to be "in or near gambling establishments" but also that the consulting work I performed was not conducive to my emotional health. In fact, the lying, cheating, and win-at-any-costs attitude I was notorious for contradicts everything Twelve Step fellowships advocate.

I did not sleep a wink that night. I had $500 in traveler's checks, and I tossed and turned in bed thinking about using that money, as well as getting a cash advance from my credit card, to build up a bankroll. *I can see it now: I'm going to relapse and kill myself in Vegas. They're going to find my body in this crummy hotel room, and Eric will be left fatherless. You have got to be the sickest, weakest person on earth!*

I got dressed and arrived early at the convention center. It was better than being in my hotel room mentally torturing myself. But even as I went about carrying out my assignment, gambling was constantly on the back, front, and all sides of my mind. This huge monkey had crawled onto my back the minute I stepped off the plane, and I could not shake it off.

I left the conference at around eleven that morning and never returned. From Monday afternoon to Thursday morning, I was playing pai gow poker and blackjack in casinos as far away from the convention center as possible. I was terrified of being spotted at the tables by anyone who either worked for my client or knew me, but coping with the pain of not gambling was even more terrifying. This was a lose-lose proposition—and one that I was all too familiar with. Thank God no one at the tables asked what brought me to Vegas.

Gamblers, especially those who are addicted and ones who do it for a living, have a way of being friendly without getting personal. We could appear to be long-lost friends without actually knowing a thing about one another. There's an unwritten code not to broach certain subjects, such as surname, marital status, family, and more intimate matters, such as whether someone is winning or losing and how a person finances their action. Now, if an individual wants to volunteer information, that's a different story, as some gamblers do like to brag (and exaggerate) on occasion, but don't expect self-disclosures to be reciprocated. Also, with the exception of poker, serious gamblers don't make too much eye contact with one another. If you think about it, most casino games are designed so the attention is focused on the cards, dice, spin of the wheel, numbered balls, and the chips being wagered and accumulated. A compulsive gambler can spend hours or even days on a casino gaming floor without making eye contact with a single soul.

Gambling in Vegas was, without a doubt, much more intense than in Tahoe and Reno combined. I could count on both hands the number of players I encountered the entire time I was gambling who stated that they were in Vegas on vacation. The rest were there for one purpose only: to beat the house or other players. They didn't make any pretense about enjoying themselves or being indifferent to the outcome. It was serious business to them.

I squeezed in an hour of gambling Thursday morning before rushing to the airport for my return flight. By the time I got up from the blackjack table, I was ahead just under $1,000 for the trip. I gave myself a pat on the back for beating Vegas. *This proves that I can hang with the big boys. And on top of everything else, my client paid me for the time I spent gambling.*

When I got home, I was disappointed that there were no phone messages from Fred or any other GA member. I spent Thursday evening and Friday writing up my report. I was afraid that my client would see through my ruse and confront me about how I really spent my time in Vegas. I was supposed to be pounding the floor of the convention center from Sunday to Thursday on their behalf. I faxed my report to Diane around three on Friday, hoping to garner some credibility for submitting my findings early. To my surprise, Diane called within an hour. For a moment, I thought she would be upset that the report was insufficient, but she was happy as a lark.

"Bill, our vice president read the report and was extremely pleased with the information you provided. He immediately asked his secretary to make copies for all the managers as well as the entire sales department. He was impressed that you were able to gather all this information in such a short time period. This is good stuff, material that we can put to use right away. The information about Quality Logic Devices (one of my client's customers), confirming that they're seriously considering switching to another vendor due to customer support issues, is invaluable. We'll make sure our account manager babysits them to ensure that they don't bail to one of our competitors. You know what's strange, Bill, is that our people who were there commented that they didn't see much of you at all. You must have been wearing a disguise. How did you do it?"

"Diane, you know I can't reveal my secrets. It's taken me years to perfect it," I replied jokingly.

I was relieved that they were pleased with my work. Yet I knew that I could have done a better job. I didn't even come close to putting 100 percent of my effort into it. Deep down, I was disappointed with myself.

The difference between a compulsive gambler like myself and the average person is that the latter would perceive the outcome in Vegas as pure luck—a fun experience—and put it out of their minds. But I should be so lucky. My delusions of grandeur kicked into high gear, and I felt this magnetic force pulling me back to the casinos. It happens every time. All forms of logical reasoning go out the window. I know that casinos don't build fancy resorts and offer low-cost buffets and free accommodations to select gamblers out of kindness and generosity. Most of them turn a hefty profit because the odds favor the house, and they cater to problem gamblers like me. I can't stop when I'm ahead, and on the rare occasions when I leave with winnings, I eventually return and give them back. My greed, lack of self-esteem, and need to self-medicate play right into their hands.

Just two days after returning from Vegas, I drove to Tahoe, believing I could continue my winning streak. The kudos from Diane had also gone to my head, and I'd fooled myself into believing that my report was reason for celebration. Hell, a compulsive gambler can always find an excuse to gamble. If my report hadn't been satisfactory, then I would have gambled because I was upset. The truth is that many of us compulsive gamblers start arguments with spouses and storm out of the house just so we can go and feed our addiction. We also tend to blame others for our problems and lack the maturity to accept responsibility for our actions.

For the next three months, I disappeared from GA and went on what would become one of the nastiest binges of my gambling career, literally spending more time in Nevada casinos than at home and going through over $53,000 in savings that I had accumulated during my nearly one year of abstinence. Meanwhile, a GA member called to inquire about my anniversary celebration, but I'm sure he, along with my home group, figured things out when they didn't hear from me following my Vegas junket. Shortly after I submitted the competitive analysis report, Micron Graphics instituted a hiring freeze and slashed their budget across the board, so my services were no longer needed. That allowed me to dive into my relapse with full force. It's as if I had eleven months of catching up to do, and I quickly made up for lost time. A common belief in GA is that when problem gamblers relapse, they don't revert to where they left off but find a way to go broke or to acquire debt to cover their clean time as well.

I can personally attest to the theory of making up for lost (gambling) time. Basically, we crash through our previous "bottom," without any indication of where our new ultimate bottom will be. I think it's a combination of releasing our repressed impulses and the triggering of our deep-rooted self-destructive tendencies. The only way I know to cushion the fall is to have a solid foundation of working the GA recovery program. At the time, I didn't qualify; I hadn't begun to work my recovery yet. I was merely attending meetings and abstaining from gambling. Looking back, I'm sure most of the other members recognized my pattern and knew where I was headed. They also knew that there was nothing they could do to stop me.

Less than a month after purchasing my Acura with cash, I turned the title over to my credit union to pay off my maxed-out credit cards and to get my hands on more gambling money. Unfortunately, I had to pay a higher interest rate because the financing was now classified as a used car loan. The loan officer was curious and commented, "It's a bit unusual for a customer to seek financing after paying cash for a vehicle. Is there a family emergency?" I just looked away and didn't even bother responding. *Yeah, there's an emergency all right—I fell off my fucking wagon.*

FIFTEEN

UNLUCKY 7s

The last bet I made in a casino was on Labor Day 1989. How ironic, considering that I would labor for the next twelve years to pay off my debt to the casino. The dramatic episode occurred during one hand of blackjack that will haunt me until the day that I die. Many experts in the field of psychology believe that traumatic events should be dealt with and put behind us, but that's where I see that psychotherapy and Twelve Step recovery differ. As we work our program in GA, we believe that it's important to remember how insidious the disease is and how reckless we can be—and boy, was I reckless that afternoon.

I had seriously considered flying to Vegas for the holiday weekend, since part of me was convinced that I should capitalize on my single winning streak there. I was also determined to win back some of the money I had been losing in Tahoe since I relapsed, so the obsession to chase my losses was stronger than any other factor. I couldn't, however, squirm out of a family obligation. My eldest sister, Mary, along with her family, was hosting a Labor Day shindig at her house on Sunday.

I felt the gambling "monkey" on my back during the entire party. More than one person asked why I kept looking at my watch. My bogus excuse was that it had been malfunctioning and I was checking on its accuracy. I ran into an old classmate I hadn't seen since high school, and we must have chatted for forty-five minutes, catching up on one another's lives over the past sixteen years. Unfortunately, I can't remember much of what we talked about. I was physically there conversing with him, but my mind was hundreds of miles away in a Nevada casino. Family members and the other party-goers had no idea that I couldn't get out of there fast enough so I could feed my addiction. To give you an idea of how strong the urges can get, many GA members disclose during their shares that when a father lay on his deathbed or a wife was in the hospital delivery room, they were out gambling. Part of the explanation for their behavior has to do with the manner in which compulsive gamblers react to stress and anxiety.

When I arrived at the casino in Tahoe around eight Sunday evening, the parking lot was packed, and I began cursing myself (and my sister) for arriving at the tail end of the holiday. The best spot I could find was at the far end of the structure. On my way up there, I kept reminding myself to peek under the hood of my Acura Integra upon my arrival, specifically to check the oil level, since the oil warning light had been blinking earlier in the day. But as soon as I applied the parking brake and stepped outside, I sprinted to the entrance. I couldn't get into the casino and start my action fast enough.

I sat down at an empty twenty-five-dollar multi-deck blackjack table that had just opened up and got on a winning streak almost immediately. Another gambler joined me shortly after my arrival, and he was a nuisance from the get-go, primarily because he was heavily intoxicated.

The man began harassing the dealer by continually asking her out for a romantic dinner, while she had her hands full trying to get him to focus on playing his cards. He was hitting on 16 and 17 when the dealer had a lousy face-up card, subsequently taking the dealer's "bust" card. He was also splitting tens when the dealer was showing a picture card. The guy only played seven hands at most, but it was painful to witness. If it wasn't for the fact that I didn't lose a single hand from the time the obnoxious guy sat down, I would have gotten up and looked for another table. I couldn't ignore the fact that this guy was bringing me tremendous luck.

After the shit-faced gambler left, I requested that the table minimum be increased to $100 to deter other amateurs or undesirable gamblers. As far as I was concerned, my winning streak thanks to the drunkard was an aberration. Increasing the minimum bet was easier than walking around a crowded casino looking for a better table. Closing off the table was also my little way of trying to convince myself and others that I was special and shouldn't be mixing with common folks. The pit boss gladly obliged. They're obviously used to eccentric players who are superstitious and compulsive about their surroundings. My winning streak lasted until around sunrise. A few other players came and went over the ten or so hours, but I was primarily playing multiple hands, heads up against the dealer. I sat at the same table, in the same chair, only getting up once to relieve my bladder, which felt like it was going to explode. I had to walk gingerly to the restroom. My empty stomach had also been growling off and on throughout the night. I started with a bankroll of $2,000, and at one point, I was ahead $17,000 (and change). I drew a small crowd from time to time, who quietly watched as I played multiple hands, wagering up to $1,000 per spot. During those moments, I was in the limelight and loved every minute of it. As far as my outer appearance goes, I was trying to act cool, but I probably looked like a zombie, which was becoming typical for me. Nevertheless, my mind was racing a mile a minute, and there was a euphoric component to it.

If I had quit right then and there, it would have been the biggest gambling win in my life. That's probably what a professional or normal gambler would do—establish a target and set a limit as to how much he or she would be willing to give back before quitting. But that's not what I'm about— never have been and never will be.

My final hand of blackjack began when a new dealer arrived. The dealer was one of the friendlier gals whom I had seen before, and it was obvious from the way she smiled when our eyes met that she recognized me as well. At the time, my winnings had dwindled down to $2,500, and I didn't feel like I was ahead by any means. On the contrary, I was desperate to retrieve the large stacks of chips that I had been playing with just a few hours ago. I began badgering myself, *You should have stopped, you should have quit. . . . Idiot! Idiot!* I didn't have the foggiest idea what time it was at that point. All I knew for sure was that my butt and back were extremely sore, and all the twisting and squirming didn't bring any relief, so I got up and played a few hands standing up. I had switched from feeling invincible a few hours before to being consumed with apprehension and uncertainty. Looking back, I was like a deer standing in the middle of the road in the wee hours of the morning, startled by the headlights of a semitruck, awaiting my demise.

"Hello, Nancy, how are you doing?"

"Very well, thanks for asking. And yourself?"

"Not too bad. By the way, I didn't notice you earlier. Where have you been hiding?"

"Oh, I just came on."

"No wonder. I'm curious . . . are you on relief duty or is this your regular table?"

"I'm working a regular shift, which means you're stuck with me here for the next forty-five minutes before I get a break," she replied half jokingly.

I was probing Nancy to determine if the pit boss was up to something. Sometimes they will attempt to snap a player's (or an entire table's) winning streak or go in for the kill by either throwing in new decks of cards ahead of schedule or by bringing in a veteran or "hot" dealer in the middle of a shift. That's why I like to know if the dealer I'm playing against is assigned to the table or a relief dealer, which is one who rotates from table to table so the regular dealers can take their breaks.

My instincts were correct. Just ten minutes after Nancy arrived at our table, a stoic-looking middle-aged man, who was wearing a fancy, ruffled white shirt complete with sleeve garters, replaced her. Nancy calmly obliged, wiping her hands and turning them over to illustrate to us that she was departing on a clean slate. I've always wondered if any dealer ever had a card or chip fall out of their hands when they did that.

Nancy picked up the red, five-dollar chip I had given her as a tip just a minute ago, tapped it near the bill slot, thanked me, and stepped away from the table. I knew that the pit boss was up to no good. Nancy didn't seem to know where to go, so she walked over to the pit boss's station. After he whispered something to her, she turned and walked toward the employee lounge. I told myself to get up from the table, but my body would not move.

I had in front of me twenty-one chips: six in $500 denominations (pink) and fifteen white chips worth $100 apiece (color schemes in most casinos have changed since 1989). Before the replacement dealer arrived, I was sitting alone at the table playing three spots (hands) simultaneously at $1,500 each. After Nancy left, I felt defiant and left my bets on the table to "ride." My competitive nature got the best of me. Removing my chips would appear as though I was scared and backing down, and I wasn't about to be intimidated.

His nametag read Skip, and he didn't crack a smile under his thick mustache the entire time he stood in front of me. *Hey, Skippy, what's up, man? Do you think you're in Vegas or something?*

He proceeded to deal from the shoe, continuing where Nancy left off, dealing the cards face up on the table. *Well, at least he didn't reshuffle the shoe.* Meanwhile, the pit boss, George, who bore an uncanny resemblance to the dealer, was now hovering over our table, standing shoulder to shoulder with Skip as though they were Siamese twins. He was staring intensely, studying my chips and cards. My first hand consisted of a 9 and a 2, while the dealer's face-up card was a 5. The pit boss had a worried look on his face.

Although I didn't have any more chips or cash to wager, George had discretion to authorize immediate credit to me as a courtesy, which is common practice in the event that an opportunity to double-down or split a pair arose for an established patron.

"Marker?" I asked.

"Go ahead," George replied.

Skip dealt one card down, sliding it under my chips. I took a peek and saw an 8 of clubs. I felt confident sitting on 19.

My middle hand displayed two aces. It was too good to pass up.

"Marker?" I repeated.

"Approved."

I expected the cards to be dealt face down, but Skip exposed two cards, one for each ace. The first card was a 3 and the second card a 4.

Not to worry. Skippy's gonna bust, anyway. At least we're taking his low cards away.

My final hand consisted of a pair of 7s: one splashed with diamonds and the other, spades.

"Can I split?" I asked the pit boss.

"Fine."

Hitting on the first 7 of spades, another 7 was dealt. This time, the suit was hearts. Without uttering a word, I just looked over at George.

"It's up to you," he commented.

"Split," I said. How could I resist? I was merely taking advantage of the dealer's face-up card. If he was showing an 8 or higher, I wouldn't have split any of the 7s. This was a windfall, as far as I was concerned. I could feel the adrenaline rush and it was invigorating. A crowd had gathered, and a woman squealed when the last 7 appeared. But this was far from over.

Lo and behold, Skip dealt me another 7 of diamonds, the fourth 7 so far. I glanced over at George. "It's your party," he announced.

"Split," I declared.

While all of this was going on, Skip had his hands full, not only dealing the cards, but also keeping track of all the money I was borrowing. George made sure that all the additional chips I requested were stacked outside of the betting circle, close to the dealer tray. So far, I was in the hole for $9,000. And that's on top of my initial wager of $4,500.

When I took a hit on the last 7 of diamonds that was dealt, it was a queen, the first picture card to surface in the hand. Moving on to the 7 of hearts, Skip dealt me a 2. I placed my index and middle fingers down on the felt table and motioned like I was flicking a piece of lint away; he turned over an 8, thereby leaving me with another hand of 17. Proceeding to the 7 of spades, I decided to study the facial expression of Skip as he slid the card out of the shoe. I didn't expect his eyebrows to flare up, but that's what happened. The fifth 7 materialized; this time the suit was clubs.

By the time Skip finished dealing cards to me, I was staring at a total of *nine* 7s as the lead cards, and the final count of each hand ranged from thirteen to twenty. Taking into consideration the fact that we were playing with six decks, there were a total of twenty-four 7s in the shoe; somehow, I ended up with over one-third of them, which is statistically outrageous. I was prepared to defy the odds, but this was not what I had in mind. My initial three hands had expanded to twelve, and the wagers totaled $19,500. The casino had fronted me $15,000, but it all happened so fast, I lost track of the markers. Everything was a blur to me. I was in such a reckless and self-destructive frame of mind that I probably would have bet my life if required. In a way, that's what I was doing. I was that far gone from reality.

From the moment Skip turned over his hole card, everything seemed to move in super slow motion. The crowd behind me must have multiplied, because the whispers got louder and less distinguishable. I had no desire to turn and face the peanut gallery. It was bad enough feeling their eyes glued on me. Suddenly, I felt like every single person in the casino was judging me. I held my breath as the card flipped and landed on the table; it was a 6, giving the dealer a count of eleven. Within a split second, I perused the table at all my cards and the sight was ominous: there were only a few picture cards visible, which meant that the shoe was rich in ten cards, increasing the odds in the dealer's favor. Still too nervous to exhale, I waited for Skip to take a hit, and the next thing I saw was a mean one-eyed jack staring right at me. I studied the 5, 6, and jack, and it was surreal. My worst nightmare was flashing before my eyes, complete with surround sound from the crowd.

I just sat there and stared at Skip's cards, while George quickly tallied up the damage. As I stepped off the stool, George was already on my side of the table, blocking my path, ready to escort me to the cashier. Skippy just had to get in one last shot. As I turned away, he said, "You have a nice day now." What an asshole.

"We'll need a check from you right away for

$15,000 to cover your outstanding balance," declared George.

Since I didn't have my checkbook with me—not that it would have made any difference, since there was less than $100 in my account—the casino had me sign one of their generic checks for $15,000, which they planned to submit to my bank first thing in the morning.

There was more bad news awaiting me in the parking lot. When I reached my new car, I noticed a fresh dent the size of a quarter just above the right front wheel well. I couldn't miss it, as the rays of the sun were hitting it dead-on, bull's-eye. It was obvious that it wasn't merely someone carelessly opening their door, but probably a compulsive gambler like myself, who lost it both inside the casino and again out in the parking lot. I should have been upset, but by then I was physically as well as psychologically numb to everything happening to me. But it wasn't the phantom vehicle that caused the real damage. In time, that dent would serve as a brutal reminder of how powerless I am over my gambling. I have chosen to accept it as the casino's farewell gift to me.

As I left the casino parking lot, I must have turned right instead of left, because the next thing I knew I was in Carson City, twenty miles east of South Lake Tahoe. As I stood at a gas station in a daze, squeezing the gas nozzle, I was tempted to continue heading east and just run away. I sat in the gas station for a while, clueless as to where I could hide, when I realized that I couldn't run away from the one thing that I despised the most—myself.

As I began navigating the twists and turns of westbound Highway 50, my mood darkened, and I became obsessed with thoughts of driving off the cliff. It seemed like the quickest and most logical solution to my problems. I was tired of struggling with my addiction, and I hated myself with a vengeance. I told myself that even GA couldn't do a thing for me. It was time to kill off the demon once and for all. There was even a bonus in the proposition: I would be free from the internal turmoil that had consumed me since I was a young boy. *Let's face it: I haven't been in control of my life; my addiction has been calling the shots all along.*

When I reached the curve where I had spun out previously, I extended my arms forward and locked my elbows, gripping the steering wheel tight at 10 and 2. Next, I stomped down on the accelerator. As I visualized my car with its new dent airborne among the giant trees, I suddenly thought of my son, who had been the one constant beam of light in my life, even throughout my addiction. I imagined Eric sitting in the front seat, conversing with me as he normally did. I thought I heard his voice whisper, *"I love you, Dad."*

I came to my senses in plenty of time to steer the car safely back into the center of the lane. But my suicidal tendencies were just temporarily halted. They would reappear at a later time, stronger than ever.

I called Fred as soon as I got home, and we had a long chat. He didn't berate me for relapsing and missing meetings, nor did he give me a lecture about GA and how I should be working the program. Fred was one of the key members in the program who participated in "pressure relief" counseling, which provides guidance to members under heavy financial pressure, including debts to bookies, bankruptcies, and even criminal charges for embezzlement. Fred has taken in members, allowing them to sleep in his office and to take sponge baths using the sink at his workplace. He also temporarily employed a number of them who had become destitute as a result of bingeing. Essentially, he had a good heart and was an excellent role model, practicing Step Twelve, which is to carry the GA message to other compulsive gamblers.

"Bill, contact the casino's collections department first thing in the morning and tell them you want to work out a payment plan," Fred advised. "Notify them that it's useless to process the check you signed since there's no money in the account. If they appear unreasonable, then throw out the word 'bankruptcy'; that should keep them at bay. Bill, the collections department is fully aware that if you file for bankruptcy, they won't see a dime of the money. As long as you're up front and prepared to honor the debt, they should be willing to work with you. And don't let them threaten you with interest or finance charges. They're generally happy just to get their money back."

When Fred brought up the subject of bankruptcy, I informed him that I was seriously considering it, in order to wipe out my debt to the casino, credit card companies, and my credit union, which by now totaled over $40,000. That's on top of the $53,000 in savings I burned through, not to mention thousands in cash withdrawals from my ATM within hours after my paycheck was direct-deposited. I was so resourceful in getting my hands on money to gamble with that I can't even give an accurate estimate of the total amount I lost during that last binge. Fred was dead set against filing for bankruptcy. He stressed the importance of taking responsibility for my actions and that making restitution was an important part of my recovery. I didn't agree, since I couldn't see the benefit of having these enormous debts hanging over me for years and years. But I would come to appreciate Fred's insight and wisdom and why it was important for me to be reminded each month, as I wrote the check and made my payment to the casino, that I am a compulsive gambler, powerless over my addiction, just as much today as I was in September 1989.

My conversation with the collections representative, as expected, was not pleasant. He pressured me to secure the money from family, friends, credit cards, and banks.

"We loaned the money to you in good faith," he said in his deep, raspy, chain-smoking voice. "You indicated from your actions that you could honor your debt. How much of the balance can you send to us right away?"

"Well, I'm flat broke and I'm currently unemployed, without any clients, and seriously considering filing for bankruptcy. Perhaps I can dig up $50 by the end of the week."

"Well, that would be a start, but we will need you to work with us to increase your payments substantially as soon as possible."

So began my twelve-year relationship with the group that would transfer my account to four different representatives, who, like clockwork, would contact me by telephone twice a year. First, they would attempt to pressure me into increasing my monthly payments; six months later, they'd offer to settle the entire debt for a lump-sum payment equal to one-half of the balance. In between, they would send nasty letters. The settlement was tempting, but Fred was against it.

"It's like a bailout, and a quick solution may lead to a relapse. You need to stretch those payments out as far as possible and think about your disease each time you write the check out and mail it to them."

After two payments of $50, I settled in on installments of $100 per month. Fred discouraged me from sending in higher payments, even when I could afford it. As I maintained a consistent pattern, albeit with low payments, the casino was, by cashing the checks, accepting the terms as though under a formal agreement. And since I wasn't paying any interest or finance charges, it was to my advantage to hang on to any extra money I had. Eventually, when I started building up my savings again, the 7 percent APR I earned on $15,000 from the bank nearly covered the monthly installments to the casino. This illustrates the mind-set as a compulsive gambler: being adept at managing money, but often for the wrong reasons.

So once a month for more than twelve years, I sat down and reminded myself of the last hand of blackjack I played. I imagined all the cards laid out on the table; the thirteen stacks of chips worth $1,500 each; Skippy and George (the Siamese twins); and most important, the out-of-control, desperate man who knew what was destructive for him but didn't have the fortitude to resist his impulses. The image served as a powerful deterrent. It would be eight years before I stepped back into a casino, and when I did, the mere thought of being there would leave me feeling extremely nauseated. A good sign.

SIXTEEN

HITTING ROCK BOTTOM

I stayed clean from September 1989 to November 1996. That's going more than twenty-six hundred days without placing a bet. I had not attained anything close to this long period of abstinence since I started gambling in elementary school. It allowed me to live something resembling a normal life. I paid my bills on time, kept up the maintenance on my car, and spent money on things for myself like clothes, decent furniture, and actual vacations where there weren't any casinos on the premises. Typically, compulsive gamblers will not spend money on normal expenditures while they're still in the grip of their disease, and this was also true in my case. It was difficult to part with money, unless it was to place a bet. Having money to get a fix had been a daily obsession of mine as far back as I could remember. To have this burden lifted felt like being released from my self-imposed prison.

When I was out there gambling, I really didn't care how I looked. I also neglected my health, nibbling on junk food to sustain myself and defying my body's need for sleep. For years, I avoided doctors and dentists. When I dropped down to around a hundred pounds after Kathy left, I brought all my suits to a tailor at a dry cleaner and asked her take in the pants and jackets. My mother could have performed the alterations, but she would have had hard proof of my deteriorating health and given me hell for it. The tailor warned me that the clothes would look awkward after she made the changes, but I really didn't care. I just couldn't see using my gambling money to purchase new suits. Holes in my tennis shoes were common; I wore them until the asphalt tore up my socks.

Growing up, my family was impoverished, so my siblings and I were raised to be frugal. You would have thought that gambling would not be tolerated in our household, where every penny counted, but that was not the case. Also, my father's alcoholism didn't deter my mother from purchasing liquor for him on a regular basis. Denial and co-dependency are powerful forces.

New members often ask me how difficult it was to stay clean during those seven years. Actually, the time passed pretty quickly. I believe hitting my bottom on that infamous final round of blackjack and being reminded of the ordeal every single month when I wrote out a check to the casino left me considerably less vulnerable to urges. Humility is probably the most important attribute in my recovery. Developing it allows me to keep my ego and insecurities at bay.

As far as GA was concerned, I didn't qualify to receive my one- or five-year pins, because I didn't meet their criteria regarding meeting attendance. Members are required to attend a minimum of thirty-nine meetings within a year in order to be recognized for their accomplishments. As far as GA was concerned, I "white-knuckled" through the seven-plus years of abstinence—meaning I wasn't working the program but was merely relying on willpower to stay clean. At the time, I didn't agree, but eventually I became one of the staunchest supporters of the rule. It prevents members from traipsing in and out of the rooms and receiving recognition, especially at pinning ceremonies. I learned the hard way that there is a huge difference between abstaining from gambling and working my recovery.

I admit that during that period, I was guilty of drifting in and out of the program, attending meetings when I felt like it—basically showing up to stroke my ego by bragging about my clean time. I truly believed that I was honoring other members with my presence. I started to believe that I was cured of my addiction. My father passed away in 1992, and I got through it without gambling. I also remarried and divorced within this time period and maintained my abstinence. Little did I know that my disease was merely lying dormant and that I was essentially a ticking time bomb, just waiting for something to set me off. And when it occurred, seven long years of repressed urges would be unleashed with a fury.

The day Eric was born was the happiest day of my life. Cuddling him in the delivery room was my proudest moment. His birth provided me with an immense feeling of redemption, as I was determined to be the best father and parent possible. My philosophy on parenting had been mapped out when Eric's mother was pregnant with him. *All I have to do is the opposite of what my parents did. Eric will never feel like he's a burden or unwanted at any time. Being his father will always be a privilege, never an obligation.* In so many ways, raising Eric allowed me to experience the childhood I never had.

Our vacations, including trips to Disneyland and Epcot Center, were as much a thrill for my inner child as they were for him.

Eric was a sweet, soft-spoken child who was never a disciplinary problem. I could count on one hand the times I admonished him for misbehaving. When Eric was eight, he *did* bring a note home from his teacher alerting me that my son was selling collectible trading cards to his classmates and making a hefty profit. The other parents complained that their children were spending all their allowances on these cards and begging for more money. The principal acquiesced to members of the PTA by instituting a rule that the sale or exchange of collectible cards was not allowed on school grounds. Kids being kids, Eric and his patrons simply completed their transactions up the street from the school. The principal responded by forbidding students from possessing these cards in school, period.

Eric cried foul and became discouraged, pleading with me to find an outlet for his entrepreneurial spirit, so we started attending comic book conventions and eventually participated as dealers. Within a year, with my guidance, Eric was running a national mail-order business out of our home.

At age thirteen, Eric got his first job working during the summer for a corporate travel company. His supervisor immediately noticed how detail-oriented and thorough Eric was in his work. By the end of his assignment, Eric was cross-referencing airline tickets and itineraries valued in excess of a million dollars. I thought it was great for them to have so much confidence in Eric, but to place such heavy responsibilities on a young teenager seemed inappropriate. But Eric said he wasn't fazed by it at all. He thought it was fun work.

As the only child of parents who divorced when he was still a toddler, I realize now that Eric often found himself caught in the middle, having to serve as both messenger and mediator for his parents. I believe that Eric's well-behaved disposition growing up was his attempt to minimize the friction between his mom and me and to accommodate my obsession for control.

At the point when Eric entered high school, his mother and I were continuing to share joint custody of him. He was enrolled in honors classes and seemed to be doing well. But it was all a facade.

When my ex-wife called and informed me that Eric had run away, I was shocked, to say the least. Eric never went out much, and now I was supposed to believe that he didn't want to come home. I had no idea that Eric was experiencing immense internal turmoil and had begun living a secret life of his own. All the years of bickering over his custody, lack of communication between his mother and me, and our conflicting styles of parenting left Eric feeling like he had no control over his life, and he was dying to break free. Running away was Eric's attempt to liberate himself from the madness of his parents' dysfunctional homes.

Over the course of the next few months, his mother and I filed numerous missing-person reports, and I spent many sleepless nights worrying about Eric's welfare. When pressed, his old friends disclosed that Eric had started hanging with the wrong crowd at school. To entice kids, organized criminal groups were using material possessions and a false sense of empowerment that parents and schools had difficulty competing against: fast cars, clothes, money, drugs, girls, protection, safe houses, firearms, and a macho image that garnered respect and popularity in the teen subculture. The opportunity to discard one's studies and adopt a new family from the dark side has always been appealing to vulnerable teens. Most are seeking a sanctuary from a troubled home life. In my case, I turned to the streets beginning at the age of seven or eight to escape psychological and physical abuse from my brother and parents. Even as crimes in the neighborhood escalated to felonies, including homicides, I still chose gang life over my biological family. There was a better chance of my being killed in the gang, but I still felt like I had more control of my life.

At first, I was worried about whether Eric was eating and had a roof over his head. But weeks would pass without any word or sightings of him, leaving me terrified that he might be dead. It's one thing if he had sought refuge at a friend's, but we had no clue of his whereabouts.

I abruptly quit all my business consulting and devoted myself to bringing Eric home. But even after Eric returned and remained at home, his relationships with his mother and me were strained. My ex-wife seemed to cope with it, but I interpreted Eric's actions as a direct rejection of me as his father and as a person. I internalized Eric's resentful attitude, and the pain was unbearable. He had been the one stable force in my life, and now I could no longer rely on our relationship to keep me together. Even though he was physically home, something inside me was screaming that I had lost him forever.

Looking back, I can see how my dependence on Eric to validate my whole existence contributed to his desire to rebel, even if it meant running away and getting into trouble with the law. I had no idea how overbearing and controlling I was as a father. During one of the episodes when Eric was detained at the police station, he told the sergeant interrogating him that he would prefer to be locked up rather than to return home with me. That should have been a wake-up call about how unhappy he was, but I wasn't mature enough to comprehend it at the time. I was shocked that my son, whom I regarded as my best friend, didn't want anything to do with me.

In desperate need for support, a close friend

suggested that I reach out to Ellen, my former therapist. I hadn't spoken to Ellen in years, but I responded that I didn't think she would be available. I don't know why I said that, but that's how I felt. When I called Ellen's office number, it had been disconnected. Then I called the Center of Attitudinal Healing across the bay in Sausalito, where Ellen worked part-time training other counselors on grief support. When I asked for Ellen, I was transferred to one of her colleagues who informed me that Ellen had passed away unexpectedly about three years earlier. She was only in her forties. The official news of Ellen's death depressed me even further, sending me scrambling to self-medicate.

Just before Eric ran away, I had achieved as much financial security as I had ever known in my life. Seven years without placing a bet allowed me to own a beautiful three-bedroom home with significant equity, numerous bank accounts with the maximum amount of savings allowed, Keogh retirement accounts, and a college fund set aside for Eric that would cover all his undergraduate expenses at a private university. Fast-forward seven months, and it was all gone—every last cent. I blew all the money away day-trading in the stock market. If you think about it, it really took tremendous skill to amass the losses that I suffered in such a short period. It was a combination of desperately seeking to escape the emotional pain, lack of discipline caused by the stress, and feeling so despondent and dejected that I set out to destroy everything that I had built up to that point. Being self-destructive was my way of rejecting myself.

Psychologically, I was hypomanic for the majority of that period. I was on edge, angry at the world, and barely slept, spending most of my time researching publicly traded companies and charting my trading strategies. I repeated the same pattern of behavior I had exhibited following my divorce, the job crisis at Advanced Circuits, and the massacre at ESL—I self-medicated by gambling. The only difference was that I didn't have to contend with long, exhausting, reckless drives to the casino or even pick up the telephone. I simply plopped myself down in front of the computer monitor and conducted all my stock trades online.

Somehow, the more transactions I made, the less control I had over my impulses. It's as if my body had gradually built up resistance, and I needed to day-trade more for the same effect. Stocks that I acquired and planned to hold for a minimum of a year were being sold off after a few days, even before the settlement date. I dumped some within an hour or two, thanks to my OCD being kicked into overdrive. A few months after falling off the wagon, I added options trading to give my fix somewhat of a turbo boost. At some point, I couldn't even fool myself into believing that I was trying to make money in the stock market; I was simply trying to stop the hemorrhaging and was chasing my losses. I have since gone back and analyzed all the transactions I completed during that seven-month binge, and it is obvious that my modus operandi was to "buy high and sell low." Someone could have made a fortune doing just the opposite.

After going through all the money, I lapsed into a suicidal depression. All the anger that I acted out by gambling was now directed inward. I was furious at myself. There was no more drug to numb my emotional pain. When what I had done finally sunk in, I began beating myself up over it, nonstop. Not only did I feel that my son had rejected me, but on top of that I'd lost everything I had worked for. I could not forgive myself for losing all that money. Money was how I defined myself: how much I made and how much I had. *You are a good-for-nothing piece of shit; totally worthless; a major fuck-up.* I went to bed each night praying that I would die in my sleep, and woke up the next morning disappointed that I was still alive. I had no desire or resolve to work. The simplest things that I used to find pleasure in, like playing tennis, reading, and watching videos, were suddenly dark and pointless. When I read, my mind drifted to faraway places. I would read a page or two and not have any idea of the contents. I picked up words but couldn't string them together. Each time I stepped onto the tennis court, all I could think of was how I was going to kill myself after the match. It was a toss-up between overdosing on trazodone, a prescription sleep aid that was in my medicine cabinet, or driving to the Golden Gate Bridge, stopping my car, and throwing myself over. Just visualizing my body sailing through the air and knowing that the deep, emotional pain would soon end produced some relief.

Even running errands became a monumental task. I would drive to the post office, a restaurant, or wherever and wouldn't be able to get out of the car. I didn't even have the energy to turn the ignition off. I'd just sit there and stare aimlessly out the windshield, sometimes for hours at a time. I was wrought with guilt and self-hatred every waking minute. Sleep offered a respite, but many dreams involved committing suicide. I also ridiculed myself for not having the nerve to take my own life. Many days, I didn't get out of bed, and if I did, I just sat mindless in front of the television. I couldn't tell you what program was on or what time it was. It was as close to being catatonic as one can get without being catatonic. The phone went unanswered and knocks on the door were ignored.

My financial dilemma only served as a reminder of what a failure I was as a man and a father. Banks that had been alerting me earlier in the year that my savings had surpassed the hundred-thousand-dollar limit for FDIC insurance were now telling me that I did not have enough funds to maintain an account. I was also ordered to close out my free safety-deposit boxes or pay the annual fees. It was an easy decision since I didn't have the money to pay the fees and I no longer had anything of value to store in them. Prior to my last relapse, I'd kept $5,000 to $10,000 in cash in these boxes, along with bank books, the title to my car, and my will. Having immediate access to cash is a habit I acquired from my gambling lifestyle. It's like a security blanket. In many ways, losing Eric's college fund was worse than losing my savings. I took considerable pride in setting aside that money for him.

After nearly two months of suffering from suicidal ideations, I made a call to my primary care physician, a wonderful, caring man named Dr. Larry Shore, and confided in him. Although he obviously had rooms full of sick people waiting due to a nasty bug going around, Dr. Shore patiently sat and listened as I poured my heart out. He gave me as much time as I needed. We talked for close to an hour and a half. He prescribed Prozac, an antidepressant that would eventually lift me out of my black hole (but cause other serious problems), and, to my surprise, he strongly encouraged me to return to Gamblers Anonymous.

Dr. Shore is an advocate of Twelve Step programs. A number of people in the medical community, including Dr. Ronald Ruden *(The Craving Brain)*, believe that individuals who attend recovery meetings can naturally raise the levels of a neurotransmitter chemical in the brain called serotonin. Dr. Shore is in this camp. Insufficient amounts of serotonin have been attributed to depression, as well as anxiety, OCD, overeating, and migraine headaches. Antidepressant medications such as Prozac are classified as selective serotonin reuptake inhibitors (SSRIs). (SSRIs don't actually raise serotonin levels but work by preventing the chemical from escaping between receptors in our brain; hence the phrase "reuptake inhibitor.") Dr. Shore believed that by returning to GA, I could get a natural boost of serotonin, which would augment the Prozac he was prescribing.

So in the summer of 1997, I dragged my butt back to Gamblers Anonymous. One day, I reached out to Fred, and he recommended that I attend a meeting that evening just a few minutes drive from my home. It was the San Francisco Friday group, which is the oldest GA meeting in northern California. Subsequently, I would adopt this room as my home group.

SEVENTEEN

SURRENDERING TO GA

After ten years of navigating through GA on my terms and paying dearly for it, I was finally ready to surrender to the program. I walked back in with my tail between my legs and announced that I really was powerless over my addiction and that I could not fight the disease alone. It's amazing how much easier it is to admit this when you're drowning and trying to grab a life preserver. Humility allowed me to accept help in the program for the very first time.

Like so many compulsive gamblers (and other addicts), giving up control and trusting others are difficult propositions for me. I have a survivor mentality. I learned at a young age that the only person I could really depend on was myself. Growing up, the people closest to me abused or disappointed me big time. But that doesn't mean I had a lot of faith in myself either, considering my self-destructive ways. Yet when gambling consumed my life and I reached a point where I would have done anything to get money to gamble, the realization that my life was out of control made it easier to surrender to the program. I had nothing to lose.

There was a period when I blamed Eric for my relapse, but returning to GA and working my recovery helped me realize that putting it on him was one of my many character defects. Eric did not open my brokerage account, nor did he encourage me to gamble in any way. He was just a teenager going through a crisis and dealing with it the best he could. How could I blame him for *my* behavior? I, on the other hand, have a lifelong history of self-medicating. I eventually had to decide whether I was ready to grow up, take responsibility, develop coping skills, and work on feeling better about myself. There were other ways to react to crises and to life in general. I just had to learn them. GA offered all of that—and more.

Things did not happen overnight. For the first month, I showed up and just absorbed what others were saying and doing. I didn't open up much during therapy because my wounds were still too raw. In many ways, I felt like a newbie, participating in the program for the first time. Even reading the

Combo Book took on a whole new meaning. Instead of questioning the text from cover to cover, I embraced the concepts and directives. Members I used to regard as losers were suddenly proclaiming words of wisdom. Several members who had come into the program the same time I did ten years earlier and had stayed clean also inspired me. I had not seen them in ages, and they appeared to be totally different people—self-confident, yet humble—with an aura of serenity. A month later, I would ask one of them to serve as one of my sponsors.

I no longer took my addiction or recovery for granted. I realized how close I had come to killing myself as a result of my gambling. I told myself that I had a terminal disease and that meetings were tantamount to a cancer patient's need for radiation treatment. Whenever I became complacent and thought of skipping a meeting, I asked myself if I would skip a radiation session if I had cancer. That always set me back on course. I also noticed that the meetings that I nearly skipped usually ended up being the most inspiring and heartfelt, thanks to newcomers sharing horrid details on how gambling had devastated their lives.

Many Twelve Steppers believe people can only begin their recovery after they hit rock bottom. That's probably true for the most part, but we need to be mindful that as addicts, there is no guarantee that we *have* hit rock bottom. All addicts are a slip away from relapse and a potentially deeper bottom. That's why as addicts, it's important to accept our addictions as lifelong diseases—we're *never* cured. People also have different thresholds for reaching their bottom. Compulsive gamblers, for example, have the highest incidence of suicide attempts (and completion) of all addicts.

I will never forget the GA meeting where a woman showed up consumed with so much guilt that she told us she'd considered killing herself. Generosa had accompanied a friend to Reno, where she said she'd gotten carried away at the nickel slot machines. Generosa had never been in a casino before. It had happened two weekends earlier, yet she described it as though it had just taken place yesterday. Generosa just couldn't forgive herself, ranting through a stream of tears that her mother did not raise her children to throw away their money like that. Generosa had no desire to return to the casino to try to win the money back, and she swore off gambling for the rest of her life. Generosa hoped GA would provide answers to how she lost control of herself. I sat there thinking, *Wow, this woman has really hit bottom.*

At the end of Generosa's share, she casually disclosed that the total sum she'd lost was $20. You can imagine the shock on the faces of this motley group. I'd never seen so many jaws drop all at once—not even in an elbow-to-elbow dice game when the shooter rolled a 7 and crapped out.

We never saw Generosa again, and when I called her a month later to see how she was doing, she said that she was doing better and becoming more involved with her church. A lot of members displayed their immaturity by laughing about how upset Generosa got over losing such a minuscule amount (they were also guilty of taking another member's inventory). One member who lost a sizable inheritance on slot machines just shook her head in disbelief, suspecting that Generosa had lost a lot more money than she let on. While it's true that most problem gamblers aren't truthful about the actual amount of money they've lost or they owe, especially to their spouses and families, they usually come clean in GA, where we commonly hear, "My wife has no idea how much 'we' really owe." It's interesting that winnings from gambling are "mine," but debts belong to "us." You can also count on the fact that compulsive gamblers who are still in action will usually have a hidden bankroll that is off-limits for anything but betting. It doesn't matter if there isn't any food in the fridge or milk for the baby; you're not going to wrestle that money away from the sick gambler.

I learned from Generosa that we all have individual bottoms, and it has nothing to do with the number of years we spent gambling or with the cumulative amount of money that we lost. I shared the same guilt and shame that Generosa felt, but it took me nearly forty years and hundreds of thousands of dollars to reach it. For compulsive gamblers such as Generosa and myself, there's really no more room to sink further. As we hear over and over again in GA, gambling for us leads to jail, insanity, or death. I consider myself lucky to be recovering from suicidal depression. For some gamblers who hit rock bottom, there is no opportunity for recovery—not in this lifetime, anyway.

Robert C. was one of the gentlest souls I encountered in the program. In his early fifties, his face showed a lot of wear and tear, yet he had a full head of dark brown hair without a trace of gray anywhere. Standing over six foot one, he looked like a waiter at an upscale restaurant. Ignoring the fact that the clothing on his back came courtesy of the Salvation Army, he carried himself in a proud and dignified manner. Robert had been struggling with dual addictions (alcohol and gambling) since he was a teenager. Recently, he had been staying in homeless shelters and working odd jobs—basically, whatever he could get. Nevertheless, he was always clean-shaven when I saw him, and he always had a dollar to contribute when we passed the collection basket around. When another member attempted to steal money by pretending to get change from the basket, it was Robert who caught him red-handed, quickly pointing out to everyone sitting at the table that there weren't any large bills collected. Robert battled his demons every minute of every day, yet he maintained high morals. I respected him for that.

Robert's revelations during therapy were powerful. He spoke frankly about the impact gambling has had on his life, including the loss of his children's respect, and how he was at the end of the road.

"If I relapse again, I don't believe I have another recovery left in me," Robert stated matter-of-factly.

The last time I saw Robert, he was approaching ninety days clean time and was on his way out of town for a job assignment. Robert informed us that he was being paid to drive a used car that had just been sold to the East Coast. He was either going to drive another vehicle back for delivery to the Bay Area, or if that didn't work out, he was going to hitchhike or catch a Greyhound bus.

Robert and I held hands as we recited the Serenity Prayer to close the meeting. I can still feel his hand gripping mine tightly and how he shook it at the end, as if he desperately needed to believe in the program and his Higher Power.

Two weeks later, I got a call from another member informing me that Robert had died. We didn't get all the details, only that on his way back, Robert had stopped in Reno and relapsed. That's where his body was found. I was a pallbearer at Robert's funeral.

Only a handful of people, all GA members, were at the service, which was organized by his brother, who worked at the funeral home.

I think about Robert a lot. I can still hear him declare that he didn't believe he had another recovery left in him. It's a shame that some people in GA felt that Robert needed to hit his bottom before he could start his recovery and therefore left him alone, waiting until he got all the gambling out of his system. But what Robert taught me is that we need to reach out and carry the GA message to other compulsive gamblers *before* they hit their bottom, which in many cases is prison, insanity, or death.

It's common knowledge that Twelve Step programs discourage major changes (life events) during the first two years of recovery. It makes a lot of sense, since the focus should be on recovery, while minimizing stress in other areas of our lives, such as intimate relationships, career, housing, and finance. Many new members don't have a choice. Their spouses leave them; they've been kicked out of the house or face eviction; their jobs are in jeopardy; and bill collectors are harassing them. Still, the main objective is to attend meetings regularly, to focus on areas of life you have control over, and to not take on too much, too soon.

Recovery programs also encourage us to be mindful of stress and anxiety, which are triggers for our addictions. The concept of HALT is familiar among recovering addicts. It warns us that being Hungry, Angry, Lonely, or Tired can leave us vulnerable to our drug of choice. I can attest that 99 percent of the time that I gambled, I was suffering from one or all of the above. It came down to learning to take care of myself, including being assertive, in order to avoid falling into the HALT trap.

It's amazing how much support and guidance a newcomer can receive from experienced members in the program. On a regular basis, in GA, we deal with individuals who are homeless, some being chased by bookies, others on trial for felonies, and many on the verge of losing their sanity. It makes a huge difference knowing that our problems are not unique and that others are fighting similar demons and contend with the same silly yet powerful delusions of grandeur. All of us had fantasies of living large and spreading our wealth to family and friends. The GA rooms are full of folks convinced that we were just one big win away from solving all our problems. We're also an impatient bunch, expecting our needs and desires to be met quickly and without much effort.

When I returned to GA, I knew I had a ton of

work ahead of me and that my experience this time around would be much different. I didn't want to repeat the same pattern of losing everything I had, then throwing myself back into my consulting business in order to get out of debt or to rebuild my savings just to slip and repeat the cycle all over again. During my last relapse, I wiped out my savings, but I stopped gambling before racking up huge debts. I guess you could call that a blessing.

At the suggestion of my therapist and with my sponsors' blessings, I took out a loan and used the money for living expenses. Not having to worry about money allowed me to focus on my recovery for the foreseeable future. Recovery entailed attending GA meetings just about every day of the week, if you include Step meetings, regular sessions with my psychotherapist, and follow-up appointments with Dr. Shore. It was the greatest gift I had ever given myself. Still, it wasn't easy convincing myself that I deserved it. I was also tempted to resume my consulting business, but my Higher Power had other plans for me, which would become apparent soon enough.

The difference in the way I turned my life over to the program and approached my recovery this time around can be summarized in three areas: service, sponsorship, and Step work.

Using my past behavior as an example, I have seen many members dodge service work. Ask a member to come in early the following week to make coffee and he'll never show up again. Nominate them for office, and they'll have a million excuses why they can't take on a little responsibility and give back to the program. I've never seen such an overly sensitive bunch of folks who don't like people telling them what to do—that includes myself at the top of the list, of course. I recall experiencing an epiphany during one meeting: *Oh my God. I'm not the only one who can't take constructive criticism or accept compliments.*

The turning point came for me as I approached my ninety-day reentry into the program, and my home group held elections at the Friday meeting for trusted servants. There were nominations for secretary, treasurer, intergroup, sponsorship, and literature. I didn't qualify for secretary or treasurer, because both of them required minimum clean time (generally six months and one year respectively), and intergroup didn't make sense since I wasn't seasoned enough to represent our room at monthly gatherings to discuss GA business. Sponsorship, which matched new members with a temporary sponsor, was a bit of a stretch, considering that whoever is in that position often serves as a sponsor himself or herself. That left the literature position, which is responsible for displaying all the books, pamphlets, articles, and handouts at each meeting. He or she is also in charge of ordering and maintaining supplies from the ISO (international service office), including anniversary key chains and pins.

Fred recommended me for literature, and there were two other nominees. The other two contenders were kind enough to decline their nominations, obviously to allow me the opportunity to be a trusted servant in the group.

At first, I didn't know what the big deal was surrounding service, but arriving early to put out the literature and ordering supplies encouraged me to accept responsibility without compensation or recognition and to put others before myself. Getting down on my hands and knees to pick up debris after the meeting was good for me as well. These small yet simple gestures provided opportunities for me to develop humility. I also made use of the phone list, calling on other members between meetings, not to talk about myself, but to inquire about how they were doing. Service work is a great antidote for being self-absorbed. I established close, healthy bonds with many members, and in some instances, we had more contact with each other than with our sponsors. Slowly but surely, through my service work, I began to see myself as a decent, responsible person. From there, I became secretary, then treasurer, relishing the responsibilities that came with each role.

It really did wonders for my self-esteem. Instead of relying on external factors such as compensation, job titles, and material possessions—all of which can be taken away at any time—for my validation, I was discovering my worth from within.

My personal opinion is that service is a good gauge of whether a member is ready (or willing) to work the recovery program. Some need a little nudge, but we have to be careful not to scare others away by bombarding them with responsibilities, especially during the first ninety days. To complicate matters, some members throw themselves into service, thereby becoming addicted to GA. They attempt to control meetings and put as much energy into the program as they did into their gambling, giving old problems a new appearance. I have been guilty of this myself. I temporarily removed myself from service while I addressed the underlying issues, such as a fragile ego, overcompetitiveness, lack of humility, and performing service for the wrong reasons.

As far as sponsorship goes, I had been the poster boy for picking passive sponsors in the past. What I needed was a veteran or two (or more) who were firm and no-nonsense about how I worked my recovery.

Essentially, I wanted to beef up what I referred to as my recovery SWAT team. That's where Ella W. came into the picture. Ella was one of the most respected GA members in the Bay Area. A quiet, petite African American woman who could have passed for Cicely Tyson, Ella founded an "open" meeting* in the 1980s—in Chinatown, of all places. Not only that, the church she rented the room from was my former parish. Talk about my Higher Power at work.

My initial contact with Ella was a bit unnerving. She chastised me on several occasions when I was disruptive during the meeting or casually disclosed

---

* The difference between open and closed meetings is that the former is *not* restricted to compulsive gamblers. Sometimes spouses and family members accompany the problem gamblers to open meetings. On other occasions, family and friends come by themselves to learn about the disease (including how they're being deceived) directly from compulsive gamblers. In open meetings, attendees may include psychology students, journalists, and anyone else interested in the subject of compulsive gambling. It shouldn't come as a surprise that many problem gamblers will not attend open meetings. They do not feel secure about the preservation of their anonymity, nor do they want to risk being judged by nongamblers. Some have also committed crimes that they can be prosecuted for and do not want to take the chance of being exposed or incriminating themselves to outsiders. And finally, for compulsive gamblers, the hope of garnering support from others struggling with the same addiction is diminished in open meetings.

something about another member. I found myself intimidated by her presence after that, similar to the uneasiness I felt around the nuns in elementary school, so I minded my p's and q's around her. But Ella ended up being the kindest, most loving person I encountered in the program. She was the one who held me when I cried my eyes out during a meeting in which I talked about Eric and how I relapsed. Ella called me regularly and encouraged me to do Step work: when there wasn't anyone to run a meeting, she said, "Bill, this is a wonderful opportunity for you to step up in the Step meeting." So I volunteered and served as secretary for the first time, arriving early to set up the room, making sure the material was distributed, and even lining up speakers to offer their perspectives on specific Steps. It was through Ella's strength, guidance, and love that I grew up in the program.

I'm a strong advocate of having multiple sponsors in the program. Some members have a sponsor specifically for Step work, which is appropriate, considering the large number of members who haven't put a lot of effort in this area. At one point, I had five sponsors, which was wonderful, since I got a lot of attention and benefited from all of their insight and wisdom. With this many sponsors, it ensured that someone would be available if I needed anything, from just a little hand-holding to support during a crisis. Securing a temporary sponsor is also recommended if you're going to travel out of town. It sure did wonders for me.

✳

In October 1997, the U.S. Tennis Association held their national team championships at the University of Nevada, Las Vegas (UNLV). I was coaching the women's open-level team out of San Francisco, and we qualified for the competition. Tennis has been a passion of mine since I was in high school, and I admit to being addicted to the sport, especially the competitive component of it. In reference to the national championships, I had only been back in GA for five months, so I was still feeling vulnerable. When the venue was announced, I had no intention of accompanying my players on the trip. No one on the team knew that I was a recovering compulsive gambler. I just told them that I had prior commitments that I couldn't get out of and proceeded to designate one of the players as the captain and coach.

During the final week of September, I started entertaining thoughts of going to the competition. It was a once-in-a-lifetime opportunity to participate in such an event, and part of me didn't want to miss out on it. (I have been competitive as far back as I can remember, whether it be in sports or everyday life—such as shining shoes, peddling illegal goods, shoplifting, and of course, gambling.) But every time I picked up the Combo Book and turned to page 17, the phrase "Don't go in or near gambling establishments" was screaming out at me in big, bold letters. I began praying for guidance, discussed it with my therapist, Andrea, and mentioned it repeatedly during my shares in GA meetings. I'm sure people around me got tired of hearing about it.

Both my therapist and Ella were supportive of me going to Vegas. Ella said, "You've come a long way, Bill. You're not the same person who tried to white-knuckle his way through Las Vegas years ago. Go and enjoy yourself at the tennis event. That's what you're going there for . . . not to gamble." Andrea said pretty much the same thing, adding, "You've worked hard in your recovery as well as in coaching the team. As long as you stay in close contact with GA members while you're there and attend a meeting or two, I don't foresee any problems."

So I called ahead and got a list of GA meetings (they're held morning, noon, and night, 365 days a year) and asked one of the secretaries, Susan, to serve as my temporary sponsor while I was there. I went over my entire itinerary with her, including the tennis schedule at UNLV. We agreed to establish and maintain regular contact as soon as I arrived Thursday afternoon.

When I arrived in Vegas and walked through the airport, the slot machines didn't bother me as they had before. I just viewed it as a sad state of affairs to exploit people that way.

Vegas had gone through a major transformation since I had been there eight years ago. As I drove through the strip in my Geo Metro rental car, new structures such as the Stratosphere, Excalibur, Luxor, and Treasure Island had been erected, with construction for the Bellatio, Mandalay Bay, and New York, New York either under way or about to break ground. The city was starting to look like one giant amusement park.

After checking in at the Flamingo Hotel, I made a beeline from the registration desk to the elevators, moving as quickly as I could along the wall, as far away from the action as possible. I did my best to block out the noise and kept my eyes away from the illicit action, but suddenly, I started to feel out of sorts. It seemed like the closer I got to the gaming tables, the more nauseated I became. My body, it seemed, had developed a negative response to the sights and sounds of gambling.

When I entered my hotel room, the red light on the telephone was blinking. There were three messages: the first was from Ella, the second from Susan, and the last message was one of my players, Ashlee, letting me know that she and her doubles partner, Roberta, had arrived together. What she didn't tell me, but I found out later, was that while Ashlee was waiting in line at the registration desk,

Roberta couldn't wait to hit the tables. By the time she was given her room key, Roberta had already dropped $1,000 in blackjack. It could have been worse, but fortunately, Roberta's aunt accompanied her and held the other $1,000 Roberta had set aside for gambling. I was tempted to have a heart-to-heart talk with Roberta about GA, but she didn't seem particularly upset about the loss, and I reminded myself that GA is a program of attraction, not promotion.

I was occupied Thursday evening with tennis business at UNLV, so I made arrangements to meet Susan at a meeting Friday evening. She and I spoke at least a few times a day while I was in Vegas, and I received calls from quite a few members from my home group. The outpouring of support from all the GA members made a huge difference. I did not experience any urges to gamble, yet the nauseating reaction I had every time I walked pass the gaming area persisted.

The Friday meeting in Vegas was intense. The common theme that I heard there was the struggle to stay clean with the action screaming out at them everywhere they turned. Many of the members who relocated to Las Vegas for business or retirement had never gambled before. A handful worked in casinos, including a few who were forced to come out of retirement after losing their pensions to the casinos. I couldn't help but wonder why most of these folks didn't just pack up and move out of the state. There was one member who was there to say farewell to the group; he was moving back to Wyoming after gambling away his life savings.

Sitting in the meeting, my heart was back in San Francisco with my home group. But listening to the Vegas GA members share their struggles of trying to stay clean while living there was an eye-opener. I realized what a big risk I'd taken by returning to the gambling mecca of the world, no matter how dedicated I was in my recovery. *How can a recovering compulsive gambler comply with the directive "Don't go in or near gambling establishments," when it's virtually in the air they breathe?* That's when I knew it was a big mistake for me to be there.

By late Saturday afternoon, my tennis team had clinched the national title by winning nine consecutive matches. I decided to leave early, so I caught the last flight back to the Bay Area, leaving Roberta in charge. My players did me proud by continuing their winning streak on Sunday, completing the tennis competition with an astonishing 12-0 record.

Susan supported my decision to cut the trip short. I thanked her for serving as my temporary sponsor, emphasizing that her watchful eye kept me out of trouble. With that said, I also told Susan that I never, ever planned to step foot in Vegas again. She understood and gracefully accepted an open invitation to be a speaker at the Step meeting that I was facilitating on Tuesdays in San Francisco.

✳

I had no idea what I was getting into when I started attending Step meetings, which is where members get together to work intensively on the Twelve Steps of recovery, one Step at a time. Through the years, I'd heard other members reference what Step they were working or stuck on and had heard announcements about certain Step meetings needing more attendance. Beyond that, I'd never paid them any attention. Upon my return to GA, I surrendered to the program wholeheartedly, and that included Step work. The fact that I was consumed with guilt motivated me to work the Steps. For new members, Step work isn't recommended until they have ninety days in the program. The therapy portion of the regular meetings tends to be awkward enough for someone new to GA, without throwing them into the fire of Step meetings.

In a nutshell, Step work is where I found the strength to forgive myself, learned coping skills to deal with everyday life issues, including stress and anxiety, and made a conscious decision to be a better person. To me, Step work is moving beyond abstinence and into recovery. Studies have shown that

GA has a dropout rate of 92 percent. Although I don't doubt that figure, I firmly believe that members who attend Step meetings and make a conscious effort to work this part of the program have a much higher rate of maintaining their abstinence.

There seem to be as many ways to tackle Step work as there are Step meetings. I'd always heard wonderful things about the treatment program for compulsive gamblers at Brecksville in Ohio and their approach to working the Steps. Unfortunately, the hospital, formally named the Louis Stokes Veterans Administration Medical Center in Brecksville, is, as the name implies, restricted to veterans. Many Step meetings have their own handouts, including forms to be completed as assigned homework. Most groups meet once a week and tackle one Step per session; others take as much time as necessary for each Step. The use of guest speakers to facilitate discussions of the Steps is also a common practice. (I have included an appendix with select notes from my own Step work.)

When I started working on the Fourth Step ("Made a searching and fearless moral and financial inventory of ourselves"), I knew that it would take extra time, but weeks turned to months of self-examination and painful confessions. In the end, all the notes and revelations I jotted down on worksheets and journals, along with a short autobiography I wrote in college, became the genesis for my book

Chinese Playground. Initially, I had no intention of sharing the secrets of my family or my criminal past with anyone. But as I proceeded to work on Steps Eight and Nine, which focus on making amends to people, it occurred to me that one way to make up for my past crimes and bad deeds was to share my story in hopes of providing guidance and support to others dealing with their own personal demons. As most writers will tell you, getting a book published is no easy feat. There is no way I would have had the strength and resolve to complete the manuscript and self-publish it without the support of my GA home group, my sponsors, my therapist, and Step work.

When the book was released, I honestly wasn't prepared for the response: the media embraced the story (with several papers printing front-page stories), reviewers raved about it, and, most important, readers loved it. Letters began pouring in from the public, both by e-mail and regular mail, and the common response was "I couldn't put the book down." My intent wasn't to keep people up all night or to get them into trouble at work, but I accepted those endearing complaints with a smile. So what began as my Fourth Step inventory and a desire to make amends became a literary project that many people embraced, especially at-risk youths who identified with the story. On more than one occasion, Ella stated that my purpose in life is to share my experiences in order to provide guidance and support to others. I'm starting to believe her and have felt her smiling down at me as I've worked on this manuscript.

No one had ever written about the Chinese underworld from the inside. My exposé was taboo and resulted in death threats against me by my former gang associates. They assumed that I was the same person they could intimidate and control. For most of my life, I felt unsafe and lived in constant fear. But my recovery from being suicidal and the strides I made in GA provided me with tremendous inner strength and conviction. I learned to trust myself and recognize my self-worth. If anything, the threats reaffirmed my will to live.

EIGHTEEN

ELLA'S LEGACY

Six months after I returned to GA, I had the honor of serving as secretary for my home group. For years, the attendance at this meeting had been averaging eight to ten people. After I took over, we saw a steady rise in our membership. Before I knew it, we were scrambling for chairs on a regular basis, as twenty to twenty-five names were recorded on the meeting log each week. Most months, after deducting for rent, coffee, and literature, we were sending anywhere from $100 to $150 to the international service office. In GA, having extra money in our coffers is discouraged, our disease being what it is. Trusted servants have been known to embezzle funds from the program. In every case that I'm aware of, criminal charges were filed without hesitation. I appreciate the fact that GA practices tough love and has clear guidelines to avoid tempting members who are still in the grip of the disease.

I was as surprised as anyone regarding the surge in our attendance. If anything, I was worried that my style would turn off some of the members and keep them away. I tend to be controlling and run a tight ship, at home as well as in my work. My worst fear early on as secretary was sitting all alone in the room. In recovery, one often hears the phrase "It only takes two people to have a meeting." Sure, I've been there and done that at other GA rooms and programs, and sometimes it *is* nice to have a cozy meeting, but I still prefer large Twelve Step gatherings. There's just more support and positive energy when more people are present. I gave it a lot of thought and concluded that there really wasn't any magic formula behind the spike in the attendance at my home fellowship. I was attending quite a few other meetings in the Bay Area and promoting my group, but other members were doing the same thing. The best explanation I could come up with for our large group size is that I simply followed the meeting guidelines and preserved the GA tradition. One way I did that was by emulating Ella's style in conducting meetings.

One of the most important things that Ella inspired me to do, as secretary, was to promote the concept that "the GA door is always open." It's common knowledge that GA has the highest dropout rate of all the Twelve Step programs. Reports I've seen have the figures at anywhere from 75 to 92 percent. I'm not surprised. In my observation, most of us in the fellowship come from troubled homes and grew up in environments that were physically and emotionally unsafe. Even housewives and senior citizens who have never been interested in gambling can suddenly develop an addiction later in life to bingo, the slots, or online casinos. The triggers can include marital problems, unresolved emotional issues, retirement and loss of livelihood, or loneliness when children leave the nest. Many come into the program emotionally immature, carrying a ton of guilt, anger, and distrust. A majority, like myself, suffer from low self-esteem and lack coping skills to deal not only with major life events but typical adversities as well. We tend to be overly sensitive, so it doesn't take much to drive us away. Sure, you always hear the phrase "Principles before personalities," but when you have other members pushing your buttons, you may find yourself contending with stronger gambling urges after attending meetings. Then there are the folks who have been arm-twisted into the room—by a judge, parole officer, spouse, psychotherapist, friend, and/or employer. They don't want to be there, and many don't believe they have a serious problem. It shouldn't come as a surprise that most don't return after they fulfill their legal requirements. Essentially, they never make it past Step One. Even for those who do admit that they're out of control, trying to convince them to give up their drug of choice by attending meetings, talking openly about their feelings, and believing in a Higher Power is a tough proposition.

"That's all fine," Ella would say, "as long as these precious souls know that GA exists and that they're always welcome here."

When members gossip about others in the program, even with good intentions, it violates the basic principles of Twelve Step fellowship. On top of taking another person's inventory, they're breaching the person's anonymity, the threat of which keeps members away from the program. If a compulsive gambler is hurting but feels that someone is spreading rumors or judging him, he will think twice about returning to GA and getting the support he needs. As far as he's concerned, the GA door is closed! Secretaries and other trusted servants cannot allow this to happen. They need to squelch this on the spot, just as Ella did with me years ago when I was out of line. If a member has the wherewithal to talk about another member, he should be encouraged to channel that energy in a positive manner by using the phone list. Over the course of fifteen years, I figure I must have made in the neighborhood of fifteen hundred calls to members just to let them know I'm thinking of them and wishing them well. For many, just knowing that someone cares can get them back to GA. It can also provide a lifeline when they hit rock bottom.

Perhaps the most important gift that Ella bequeathed, not only to me but to the entire Bay Area GA family, was being a stellar role model. Ella didn't always speak during therapy. When she did share details of how gambling used to consume her life, it was out of concern for a new or troubled member and not just to hear herself speak. On many occasions, she sat alone at the Chinatown meeting and read the Combo Book aloud to herself. She wasn't fazed by the lack of attendance. Ella wanted to be there just in case someone needed a meeting. In the meantime, she and her Higher Power carried on the tradition. It's no coincidence that the meeting Ella founded was an "open" meeting. In addition to offering support to problem gamblers, she provided guidance to their spouses, family members, and friends. In recovery lingo, we say that Ella "walked the talk."

Ella passed away on the morning of September 28, 2002. I never knew her exact age, but what I do know is that she had been in recovery from gambling for over fifteen years.

EPILOGUE

I relapsed in September 2001. A number of factors contributed to it, beginning in 1999. My relapse while working the program illustrates how insidious the disease is and how vulnerable addicts are and will always be.

In November 1999, a former client called and offered me a consulting gig. The chief executive, John Chang, and I had worked together for many years, and he was heading up a new Internet firm in Silicon Valley, where the dot-com boom was in full swing. I had some reservations, but I fooled myself into believing that I would limit myself to working just eight hours a day, five days per week. But once I got into the assignment, I fell back into my old ways. Although I was billing the company for forty hours per week, I was working seven days a week and putting in twice my billable hours—feeding my dual addiction. It was a combination of getting caught up in the action, a desperate need to please John, and a convenient way to self-medicate.

In late 2000, my client made preparations to acquire a firm back east. My due diligence uncovered major flaws with the targeted company's core technology, and my client was able to walk away from the deal just in the nick of time. I received plenty of kudos, along with bonus stock options, and it all went straight to my head. I ended up with more than just an inflated ego; my delusions of grandeur were triggered, and I started to believe that I could do anything, including invest in the stock market again.

Around Christmastime, I received a call that Ella had been rushed to the hospital, where she was treated for dementia and diabetes. Subsequently, she was moved to a convalescent facility, where she was placed on a restricted diet. I no longer lived in the city, but I visited Ella at least once a week, bringing her one of her favorite foods, baked pork buns. Of course, I had to clear the treat each time with the nursing staff.

A few other GA members also visited Ella, and they commented that Ella often didn't recognize them and was confused about her surroundings. I prepared myself for this every time I walked into her room, but she always knew who I was and recalled vivid details of our conversations from months and even years ago. Nevertheless, I knew I was visiting her as my friend, and not as my sponsor; I didn't want to burden her with my issues. Unfortunately, I was no longer communicating with my other sponsors on a regular basis. For some reason, after Ella was hospitalized, instead of turning to others in the program, I pushed my other sponsors away, as though I were afraid they might also become ill or die on me. This goes back to my unresolved issue of being abandoned and rejected as a child.

I spent most of 2001 contending with strong gambling urges even as I remained active in GA. As the year progressed, the amount of stress in my life increased, resulting in stronger desires to gamble. I was feeling the void of Ella as my sponsor, worried about her health, and fully addicted to my work. I was gradually sleeping less and less, and my moods primarily consisted of being impulsive, impatient, easily agitated, and hostile. In psychological terms, I was alternating between being hypomanic and outright manic. Often, thoughts would be racing in my head and I'd be speaking at a frenetic pace.

It didn't help that I switched health plans beginning in 2001 and no longer had access to my former psychotherapist. There was an eight-week waiting period at my HMO to see a counselor, even when I informed them that I was in crisis. I finally got in to see my internist, and after disclosing my anxieties and impulses to gamble, the doctor responded by increasing the dosage of my antidepressant medication. The result was that it disrupted my sleep further and left me more aggressive, more temperamental, and needing to self-medicate even more. (Studies have shown that compulsive gamblers who were prescribed an SSRI medication experienced some relief from gambling urges. I think it makes sense if the individuals are suffering from OCD. But for many gambling addicts like myself who are also manic depressive, SSRIs can aggravate the mania, triggering gambling urges and violent behavior, as well as suicidal depression.)

In hindsight, I should have sought out Andrea, my former therapist, and paid for the sessions out of my own pocket. I'm also convinced it would have made a huge difference if I had consulted a psychiatrist who specialized in treating addictions. Any competent pdoc (psychiatrist) would have recognized my symptoms and, along with my history, arrived at the correct diagnosis: bipolar II (manic depressive), with OCD and PTSD (post-traumatic stress disorder). Even with my counseling background, I always associated bipolar illness with individuals who had wild mood swings between euphoria and depression, hallucinations (imagining voices and sounds), delusions (fearing someone is out to control or hurt them), and psychotic episodes. Since I didn't experience these symptoms, I overlooked the milder mood disorder—bipolar II, also known as soft bipolar.

In 2003, when I reviewed the characteristics of manic depression (bipolar disorder) and completed a questionnaire to identify the illness, I was amazed at the similarities with the text of the GA Combo Book, including the twenty questions. Both diseases involve delusions of grandeur, engaging in reckless activities, ability to function without sleep, bouts of irritability and anger, overwhelming feelings of guilt and worthlessness, isolation, and suicidal ideations. I now realize that manic depression plays a key role in my gambling addiction. Since my diagnosis, I have become acquainted with many others suffering from bipolar disorder who are also compulsive gamblers. Difficulty controlling impulses—especially as stress and anxiety increase—is prevalent among bipolar sufferers. In addition to (or in place of) gambling, many people who have bipolar disorder are also cutters (self-mutilators), shopaholics, or sex addicts.

I came across a University of Minnesota study in which compulsive gamblers were successfully treated with naltrexone, a drug first used in 1984 to treat heroin addiction. In 1995, the FDA approved naltrexone as an adjunct drug to help alcoholics control their urge to drink. Low dosages of naltrexone have also been attributed to killing cancer cells. In the Minnesota study, three-quarters of the participants given naltrexone stated that their symptoms (gambling urges) were much improved. I have discussed this with my psychiatrist, and we have an understanding that naltrexone will be prescribed for me if my gambling urges become overwhelming. So far, I haven't needed it.

✳

I remain a strong advocate of GA and believe it is an essential component of a compulsive gambler's treatment plan, in addition to psychotherapy and non-addictive medication (if warranted). I believe all individuals with a gambling problem can benefit from attending meetings, working with a good sponsor, performing service, and doing Step work. I know of some members who stopped attending GA meetings but became more active in their church, and that works for them. I think it's important for all problem gamblers to be evaluated by a psychiatrist. The stigma may be a deterrent, but the correct diagnosis could very well be a lifesaver. Identifying or ruling out OCD, anxiety, impulse control disorder, cross-addictions, and bipolar disorder is imperative in arriving at the appropriate treatment plan.

Keeping a daily journal is highly recommended, both as a cathartic tool and to remind each of us how devastating our addiction can be. For some strange reason, compulsive gamblers with amazing abilities to retain information have short memories about the pain and anguish they suffer at the hands of their disease.

In my experience, 99 percent of those who walk into their first GA meeting are financially devastated and mainly seeking help to abstain from gambling. That's fine initially, but recovery is much more than controlling urges. It's a combination of learning about our disease and transforming our lives to become good, decent people. I was able to abstain for many years without working the program, but I was merely a ticking time bomb. When I see new members come into the program, I know that it's not realistic for them to trust a group of strangers, especially a bunch of self-professed liars, thieves, and hustlers. Most of the members I have encountered in my fifteen years in the program disclose a history of childhood abuse—be it verbal, physical, or both. Some abuses are very subtle, such as unrealistic expectations for the member to succeed in sports or in school.

For spouses and family members of gambling addicts seeking guidance, I strongly recommend attending Gam-Anon and open GA meetings. All available resources will be needed, including direct input from other compulsive gamblers, in order to uncover the addicts' secret lives and to institute damage control. Often, when these folks review bank statements, request a credit report, examine their tax returns, or discover a private post office box, they're shocked to uncover the secret life the compulsive gambler has been living. Unfortunately, all too often, addicts drag their spouses into debt and even bankruptcy. It's no wonder that wives and children of problem gamblers have a higher incidence of attempting suicide than the general population.

I'm still learning about things that not only trigger but also enable me to gamble. Money has always been a sensitive issue for me, and I'm still learning about the different ways it gets me into trouble. I have to be especially mindful when I'm making good money, accumulating it quickly, or just have it socked away in a savings account. I grew up validating myself through money, and like my parents who argued day and night over the lack of it, I placed too much emphasis on it. The end result is that I lose my perspective and, like a kid in a candy store, mishandle it (by gambling). The prudent thing for me and many other compulsive gamblers to do—whether we like it or not—is to turn our finances over to someone we can trust: a spouse, family member, sponsor, accountant, business manager, or attorney. In return, we get living expenses, very much like a child who receives an allowance. We may resent it, but it's for our own good.

Competing in sports is also unhealthy for me. I place too much emphasis on winning, especially on the tennis court. I relied on winning to validate my self-worth and was so desperate to be victorious that

I resorted to cheating even during practice matches. I finally gave up on participating in tennis tournaments and now only play for exercise.

Another one of my triggers has to do with the fellowship. I have had ongoing problems with other members violating my anonymity in the program, and that has kept me away from GA from time to time. There are also plenty of members who only "talk the talk." When I find it difficult to "place principles before personalities," I attend other Twelve Step fellowships. But no matter which meetings I attend or which treatment plan I follow, I continue to strive to integrate the principles and directives of GA into my daily life.

I'm ashamed to admit that just before I hit rock bottom, I turned to the devil and offered my soul in exchange for a winning streak. Now I realize that he already had it, and that God was working to salvage it. I just needed to let him do his work.

APPENDIX A

STEP WORK NOTES

For readers interested in how I formulated my responses, the comments, which are self-contained, correspond to the text from the GA Red Book *(A New Beginning)*. The book is usually for sale at GA meetings and may be ordered directly from the Gamblers Anonymous International Service Office in Los Angeles. [*]

---

[*] The Twelve Steps of Gamblers Anonymous are also found in *Gamblers Anonymous* (Combo Book), revised October 2003, 4–5. They have been reprinted with permission.

Step 1. We admitted we were powerless over gambling—that our lives had become unmanageable. For the first ten years of my membership in GA, I admitted openly that I was powerless over gambling, but deep down, I was still in denial. My delusions of grandeur included dreams of getting on a winning streak, which would solve all my problems. Giving in to the concept that I was powerless over something meant that I was weak, and my ego could not accept that. I lost track of how many times I swore I would never gamble again, only to succumb to the urges. After years of abstinence, I wanted to believe that I could gamble normally, but that only proved that I didn't accept how powerless I really was over gambling.

It helped for me to write out in detail all the damage gambling had caused in my life and to answer the Twenty Questions in writing. Putting all this down on paper was a lot harder than just talking about it time and time again in meetings. Reading about all the harm I brought onto myself was gut-wrenching but emotionally therapeutic. It's harder to deny it when you see the proof staring out at you in your own handwriting—just like the monthly checks I wrote and sent to the casino for twelve years.

Step 2. Came to believe that a Power greater than ourselves could restore us to a normal way of thinking and living. While many new members express their skepticism regarding a spiritual force, I recall one member who struggled for months because he didn't believe in God or any other spirit. But he knew he was helpless over his addiction, so he picked the doorknob in our room as his Higher Power. Eventually, he shifted his focus and designated the meeting as his "HP," which many members do. Still others regard their sponsors as their HP, which may be acceptable for the short term, but is generally discouraged because each and every member is vulnerable, and an HP should be a constant force. I would never allow a sponsee to rely on me as his HP, because it would be disastrous if I relapsed, which is always a possibility in recovery.

For most of my life, I believed in God, so it was natural to accept him as my HP. But there were times when I was growing up that I was mad at him, blaming him for my problems and feeling that he had abandoned me. But I wanted to alter my thinking, and told myself that my HP loves and cares about me. Feeling like I deserved to be restored to a normal way of thinking and living was a big part of allowing my HP to help me. My home group also served as my HP; the environment there evolved to the point where I felt physically and emotionally safe there. It was the first time I experienced this in my life.

Step 3. Made a decision to turn our will and our lives over to the care of this Power of our own

understanding. Statements in the Red Book on this Step really hit home with me. They point out things that happen that may appear to be coincidences, but could be the work of our HP. I reflect back on my car breaking down on the way to Reno, how I ended up being at ESL when the massacre occurred, and many other spiritual experiences that I've had. Instead of accepting my calling and God's presence, I used to think I was cursed and considered myself to be the Grim Reaper, working on behalf of the devil.

The one thing that I've learned about God is that we don't have all the answers about his intentions and what he's responsible for. I was raised Catholic, and when God is seen as the Almighty, it's natural to point fingers at him when bad things happen. For instance, we can talk about the miracle that occurred at ESL—where so many escaped Farley's gunfire—but what about the victims? Did they not deserve to be part of the miracle? And if I was deemed a hero, did God show his appreciation by allowing me to relapse?

As I work Step Three, I remind myself that I am not alone and that progress may be slow. Also, this Step motivated me to change my perspective on money. My lifelong chase of money to define my worth came to an end. Having wealth has not brought me happiness. It is definitely not synonymous with serenity. In 1999, when I sold my home, I gave away most of my possessions. That included furniture, appliances, and all my business attire. Simplifying my life allowed me to free myself of material objects and to strive for spiritual wealth.

Step 4. Made a searching and fearless moral and financial inventory of ourselves. In my opinion, this is the toughest Step to work on, because if one is not careful, it can open up a Pandora's box, stirring up a lot of guilt. I discovered that my own moral and financial inventory began even before I was born, when my parents attempted to abort my birth. The realization that they considered selling me was also very painful to revisit. And since I grew up on the streets, committing crimes to survive and for gambling money, there was a lot of area to cover, especially since my gambling spans over forty years. Considering how difficult it was to admit all my mistakes and the path of destruction I left behind in my life, it was extremely painful to deal with the harm I had caused myself.

The Fourth Step is quite an undertaking; many members start on it and then move on, returning to it as they peel back layers and layers of protective emotional scar tissue. This Step is a good example of why Step work is done over and over again: we're continually evolving.

Step 5. Admitted to ourselves and to another human being the exact nature of our wrongs. I consider myself fortunate since my psychotherapist at the time was available to me throughout the period I engaged in Step work, and she did her best to keep me from falling into the guilt trap during and following my Fourth Step inventory. My therapist was also extremely supportive of the efforts I made to expand my notes into a memoir.

Step 6. Were entirely ready to have these defects of character removed. The first time I worked on this Step, there were five of us in the room. We began by listing our character defects, and while the other members were done writing after five to ten minutes, I was just getting warmed up. They started getting restless as each time I placed my pen down and they were ready to begin discussing the Step, I'd start scribbling again.

It became apparent to me that I relied on many negative traits, such as egotism, arrogance, false pride, and conceit, to compensate for my insecurities. And I wasn't sure I was ready to let go of them. Other character defects were attributes that I developed at a young age in order to survive; they include anger, bigotry, hatred, distrust, profanity, revenge, dishonesty, violence, and aggression. At some point, it dawned on me that these characteristics are also triggers for my gambling. My arrogance and inflated ego relished being treated like a casino VIP, while my compulsion to return to win back my losses was essentially an act of revenge. It reached a point where I directed the anger, hatred, and violence inward, where it manifested into self-loathing and suicidal ideations.

Instead of attempting to rid myself of the character defects all at once, I worked on one or two at a time, using meditation as a tool to stay mindful of both my behavior and my response to conflicts.

Step 7. Humbly asked God (of our understanding) to remove our shortcomings. My biggest challenge with this Step was putting my trust in someone, and that included my Higher Power. I have always been terrified of rejection. Growing up, when I prayed and didn't get a response or the results I desired, I interpreted it as God ignoring me. I convinced myself that I didn't deserve his attention. Other times, I assumed that he was upset at me for the crimes I committed. Trusting him to remove my shortcomings was also terrifying, since many of my character defects had served as emotional shields. When I hit rock bottom, I realized that I couldn't do it alone— and that I deserved *recovery*. I desperately wanted to trust someone, and what better person to surrender to than my Higher Power?

Step 8. Made a list of all persons we had harmed and became willing to make amends to them all. Where to begin? I started by recounting people I had harmed as a direct result of my gambling. It was easier for me to list them starting with the most recent. As suggested in the Red Book, I placed my name at the top. There were many people I was verbally abusive to as a result of being a compulsive gambler and sore loser. These included my son, friends, clients, job applicants, former employers and girlfriends, tennis opponents, fellow gamblers, store clerks, gas station attendants, brokerage firm and casino employees, neighbors, other drivers on the road, restaurant servers—the list goes on and on. As I worked my way back on the timeline, there were many people I had harmed in the course of being a street criminal and gang member, people I stole from, bullied, cheated, and physically assaulted. Finally, the last group consisted of people who had harmed me; this list was also quite extensive. Admittedly, there were people that I regarded as evil that I couldn't easily forgive. I knew it hurt me to carry grudges against them, but I'd be lying if I said I was able to wipe the slate clean with everyone. But my goal was to forgive at least one person each time I worked on this Step.

Step 9. Made direct amends to such people wherever possible, except when to do so would injure them or others. In both regular and Step meetings, I've heard members talk about making amends and how it blew up in their faces. In some of these instances, it was quite obvious that the members were more concerned with getting rid of their own guilt than the welfare of the people they had harmed. Alas, their experiences motivated me to question my own intentions in making amends. I needed to factor in the effect my actions would have on past victims. If I thought that certain individuals would not welcome contact from me or have no desire to rehash old issues, then I would make amends anonymously or redeem myself in other ways. I found that volunteering my services or lending a hand to friends, acquaintances, or even strangers were great alternatives. Sometimes my Higher Power lent a hand as well.

I used to make a habit of jamming parking meters when I didn't have enough change or just felt like getting away with something. This was one of the items I listed when I was working on Step Eight, which for me involved harming not only people but businesses as well. What baffled me was how I was going to make amends to the Department of Parking and Traffic Control. Suddenly, in a six-week period, I received four parking citations, all as a result of faulty parking meters. Upon receiving the first ticket, I wrote down the time, location, and meter number and was prepared to contest the citation—but then it became apparent to me that my Higher Power was at work. *If this is the case, then other citations will follow.*

And so they did, and I paid all the fines in a timely fashion. I also reported the malfunctions anonymously in consideration of other drivers.

Step 10. Continued to take personal inventory and when we were wrong, promptly admitted it. The Red Book encourages taking daily inventory and mentions the slogan "One day at a time." Since I learned in my own recovery that it is best to take things a moment at a time, that's what I strive for in my personal inventory. Throughout the day, I aim to be mindful of my thoughts and actions. Helping another person is actually easy to carry out. But what's more challenging for me is my response when I've been offended by someone. It could be a rude worker at a deli or a driver on the freeway consumed with road rage. In the past, I would be hostile and confrontational. But catching myself and then assessing the situation allows me to take inventory of my feelings, which is usually fear manifesting itself as anger. Instead of yelling at the deli clerk or demanding to speak with the manager, I practice kindness toward them (as well as to myself) by keeping calm and just focusing on what I want (and deserve). If it's not possible for them to serve me in a professional, dignified manner, I'll just seek out another worker or take my business elsewhere. As for the driver acting out, I've been there and done that more times than I can recall. Now I tell myself that

I'm just encountering other drivers who represent the old me, and I raise my arm up like a white flag, refusing to engage in "metal" or mortal combat with them.

Step 11. Sought through prayer and meditation to improve our conscious contact with God as we understood Him, praying only for knowledge of His will for us and the power to carry that out. There was never any doubt in my mind that my Higher Power is God. For those who practice other religions, their HP takes different spiritual forms. GA actually helped me get reacquainted with God. I stopped trying to negotiate and to hustle him. I also had to stop blaming him for my troubles, including my addiction.

I wish I didn't have to hit rock bottom before I was willing to accept God's hand, but that's the path my ego chose to take. Service in the fellowship and Step work were opportunities for me to get closer to my HP. I regard the other tools and resources available to me, such as psychotherapy and medication, as gifts from God.

Prayer also takes a whole new meaning for me. It's no longer about asking God for something, it's about sharing our daily life with him and the revelation of the Serenity Prayer at that given moment. Prayer also allows me to let my guard down and reveal my vulnerabilities to my HP.

Step 12. Having made an effort to practice these principles in all our affairs, we tried to carry this message to other compulsive gamblers. When I became secretary of a meeting for the first time, at the San Francisco Friday night group, I had no idea that it would provide numerous opportunities for me to practice the Twelfth Step. The position required me to arrive early to make coffee, put out snacks and set up the room, welcome new members who were checking the program out like wounded animals suspicious of unfamiliar surroundings, share my story, use the telephone list, and visit sick members.

I have always admired proactive sponsors who go the extra mile for their sponsees. Many will drive great distances just to pick up members and take them to meetings. It was inspiring each time I witnessed this, and eventually some of it rubbed off on me.

After Ella was transferred to a convalescent facility, I made arrangements with the nurses to take her out for meetings. Then when it became difficult for her to walk even short distances, a few members and I brought the meeting to her, using the dining room on her floor for our gatherings. Other times, Ella and I held meetings with just the two of us reading the Combo Book in her room.

I'm honored to have this opportunity to share my story with the public. The publication of this book is another medium for me to practice Step Twelve.

APPENDIX B

DIRECTIVES FROM THE GA COMBO BOOK*

1. Attend as many meetings as possible, but at least one full meeting per week. **MEETINGS MAKE IT.**
2. Telephone other members as often as possible between meetings. Use the Telephone List!
3. Don't test or tempt yourself. Don't associate with

---

* This material has been reprinted from *Gamblers Anonymous* (Combo Book), revised October 2003, 17. It has been reprinted with permission.

acquaintances who gamble. Don't go in or near gambling establishments. **DON'T GAMBLE FOR ANYTHING.** This includes the stock market, commodities, options, buying or playing lottery tickets, raffle tickets, flipping a coin or entering the office sport pool.

4. Live the Gamblers Anonymous Program **ONE DAY AT A TIME.** Don't try to solve all your problems at once.

5. Read the **RECOVERY** and **UNITY** steps often and continuously review the Twenty Questions. Follow the steps in your daily affairs. These steps are the basis for the entire Gamblers Anonymous Program and practicing them is the key to your growth. If you have any questions, ask them of your Trusted Servants and Sponsors.

6. A Pressure Relief Group Meeting may help alleviate legal, financial, employment and personal pressures. Adherence to it may aid in your recovery.

7. Be patient! The days and weeks will pass soon enough, and as you continue to attend meetings and abstain from gambling, your recovery will really accelerate.

ABOUT THE AUTHOR

Bill Lee was born and raised in San Francisco. He is the author of *Chinese Playground.* He has written for the *San Francisco Chronicle, AsianWeek,* and numerous professional journals. Lee has more than twenty years of experience in corporate employment, executive search, and management consulting. He has been featured on The History Channel, Fox, and A&E Television Networks. You can visit his Web site at www.chineseplayground.com.

Hazelden Publishing and Educational Services is a division of the Hazelden Foundation, a not-for-profit organization. Since 1949, Hazelden has been a leader in promoting the dignity and treatment of people afflicted with the disease of chemical dependency.

The mission of the foundation is to improve the quality of life for individuals, families, and communities by providing a national continuum of information, education, and recovery services that are widely accessible; to advance the field through research and training; and to improve our quality and effectiveness through continuous improvement and innovation.

Stemming from that, the mission of this division is to provide quality information and support to people wherever they may be in their personal journey—from education and early intervention, through treatment and recovery, to personal and spiritual growth.

Although our treatment programs do not necessarily use everything Hazelden publishes, our bibliotherapeutic materials support our mission and the Twelve Step philosophy upon which it is based. We encourage your comments and feedback.

The headquarters of the Hazelden Foundation are in Center City, Minnesota. Additional treatment facilities are located in Chicago, Illinois; Newberg, Oregon; New York, New York; Plymouth, Minnesota; and St. Paul, Minnesota. At these sites, we provide a continuum of care for men and women of all ages. Our Plymouth facility is designed specifically for youth and families.

For more information on Hazelden, please call **1-800-257-7800.** Or you may access our World Wide Web site on the Internet at **www.hazelden.org.**